MATERIALS
INNOVATION & DESIGN

LINKS

MATERIALS: INNOVATION & DESIGN

Author: Dimitris Kottas
Editorial coordination: Jacobo Krauel
Graphic design & production: Dimitris Kottas
Collaborator: Oriol Vallés, graphic designer / Roberto Bottura, architect
Text: Contributed by the companies, edited by Jay Noden

© LINKSBOOKS
Jonqueres, 10, 1-5
08003 Barcelona, Spain
Tel.: +34-93-301-21-99
Fax: +34-93-301-00-21
info@linksbooks.net
www.linksbooks.net

Printed in China

MATERIALS
INNOVATION & DESIGN

LINKS

Introduction

Materials have always affected architectural practice. Traditional architecture was always determined by the availability of materials like stone, wood and clay. For centuries most buildings were made using locally available materials. Materials were rarely imported from faraway sources, a practice which only took place for the most luxurious of buildings. This situation changed in the 19th century with the introduction of industrially produced materials, like iron, steel and concrete. These materials played an important role in the emergence of modernism. All of them were, at first, accepted for their technical properties and were used only in structures with high technical and low aesthetic demands. It took the genius of many architects and designers for the aesthetic potential of these materials to be discovered.

Today the situation is radically different. Architects no longer need to adapt their ideas to a limited availability of materials. It is possible to find materials with almost any desired properties and even to manufacture certain materials and elements with specific properties on demand. This greater freedom brings greater responsibility for the designer; he or she needs to be informed and to be able to make the right choices. Apart from the technical and expressive potential of the material, many other factors should be considered: the impact of the material on the environment, the ease with which it is handled, its maintenance and the possibility of its recycling after use, among others. Below we offer a summary of the various trends and ideas that form the landscape of contemporary architectural materials.

Ecology and sustainability

The days when sustainable building meant greenhouses in single family homes are long gone. Today the field of sustainability has been expanded and encompasses the whole process of building construction, use and eventual demolishing. Greater demands on sustainability from both the state and users and many technological advances have made the issue the center of focus for many projects.

In the field of materials there are many aspects to be considered. First of all it is the life-cycle of the material itself. The production of a material can use a bigger or smaller amount of resources and energy and may or may not create toxic and pollutant by-products. Reclaiming materials from old buildings is an ancient practice that has been re-invented in the field of design materials. Materials with a great content of post-consumer recycled content, although not always of the highest technical standard, can be very effective in various applications. Recycled materials usually have uneven colors and textures but many designers

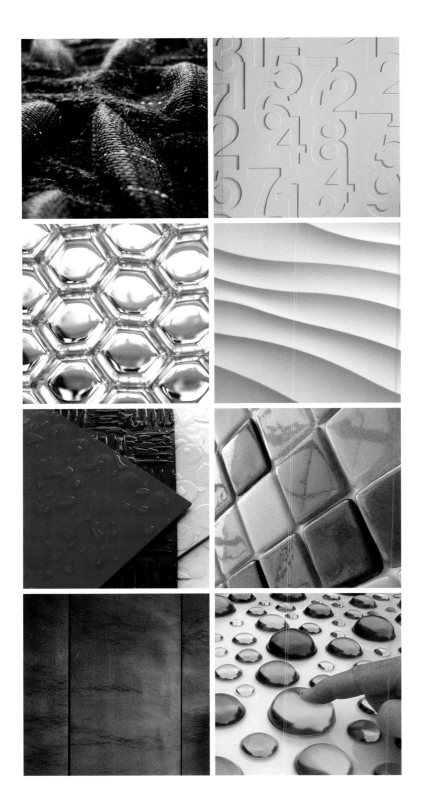

and companies have seen this as an advantage since it gives the materials a unique appearance. Bio-based materials, from plant products and agricultural waste, are also becoming common and many of them offer exciting design possibilities.

The overall energy consumed in the production process and transportation of a material until it is used on a construction is called embodied energy. Although notoriously difficult to calculate accurately, embodied energy can be used as an index for a material's impact on the environment.

Also, during the building's use, materials can have beneficial or harmful effects on the environment. Avoiding materials that emit toxic substances even below the allowed levels is practiced by many designers and such materials are increasingly being made available by manufacturers.

The last step of a material's lifecycle, its disposal after renovation or demolition, should also be considered. Many companies offer products that are purely biodegradable while other products may be dismountable and reusable. Of course, sustainability is not just about minimizing harmful effects; many materials can have a positive influence on the building's ecological performance. The preference for glass buildings has created a problem of insulation and sun protection that has been addressed by many materials. Aerogel is an example of a transparent insulating material, while translucent insulation is also available. Energy harvesting has made many advances from commercially available flexible solar cells to experimental proposals of great interest.

Nano- and Smart materials

Material technology has advanced greatly over recent years and many materials that at first sight seemed to come straight out of a science fiction film are readily available on today's market. A nanometer is one millionth of a millimeter or $1 \times 10\text{-}9\text{m}$. This is the scale of large molecules and DNA. Fabrication of materials at that scale, by determining the exact position of each molecule, enables the creation of materials with properties enhanced by 500 times or more. Although the technology is not always commercially viable there are some materials already available. Nano-engineered surface coatings that repel dirt, for example, have become available for many materials. Smart materials are materials that react to specific changes in their environment by changing their properties. Such a reaction in smart materials is immediate, predictable and completely reversible. Shape memory is one illustrative property. Shape memory alloys and polymers can change their shape under the influence of heat or electricity. Such change is always discrete and predictable (the material changes to a specific form at a specific temperature), immediate and reversible (the material returns to its previous form after the stimulus is removed without being damaged or fatigued by the change). Shape-memory is more commonly used in situations of precise micro-engineering, like medical implants and seldom if ever in construction. However, Japanese designers Nendo have made very creative use of a shape memory alloy for their lamp Hanabi. Much more common materials in that category are those that change their color or transparency with the application of heat or electricity. Thermochromic materials (materials that change color when affected by heat) have been used to make sunglasses and thermometers and (more creatively) by architects like Jurgen Mayer H. For glazed building surfaces electrochromic glass is preferred because its color can be more directly controlled by electricity and does not depend on weather conditions. Suspended particle displays are a different form of smart material that produces the same effect.

More common in architectural practice are energy-exchanging smart materials. These materials remain unaffected themselves by energy inputs but are able to transform the energy from one form to another. Solar cells, fluorescent materials and LEDs all belong to this category and are widely used today for energy conservation and harvesting.

Responsive architecture

For many centuries buildings have been mostly static. Today it is possible to design buildings that respond to changes in the environment or to human gesture. One of the first attempts was Jean Nouvel's Institut du Monde Arabe constructed from 1981 to 1987. The light-controlling façade was designed to react automatically to changes in the natural light. Later the Tower of the Winds by Tadao Ando was also designed to react to weather changes.

Every responsive system has two primary components, a sensor and an actuator. A sensor is the part of the system that monitors the environment and gives the signal for the reaction to happen when it detects specific stimuli. The actuator is the part that receives the signal and makes the change happen. Of course it is possible to create responsive systems from common elements like thermometers and electric motors but the use of smart materials and/or electronics can make such systems much smaller and more sophisticated in their ability to discern signals and react. Photochromic materials, for example, are an elemental form of a responsive material. Energy-exchanging smart materials can be used as sensors or actuators for more complex systems. Photovoltaic and thermoelectric materials can be used as sensors and they

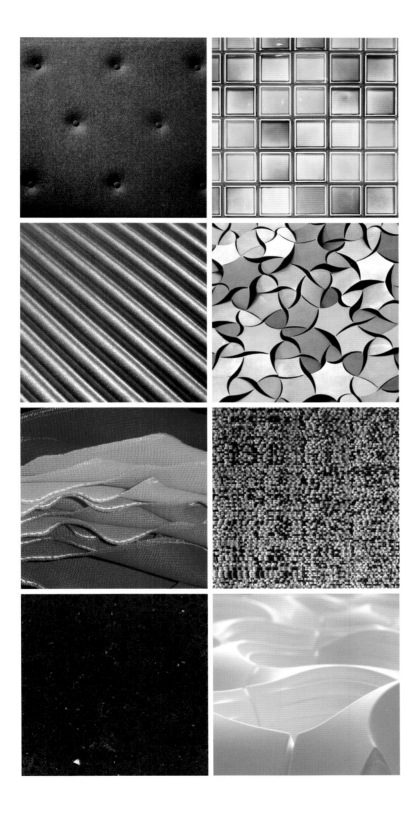

can be connected to piezoelectric or shape-memory materials as actuators. By introducing a computer between sensor and actuator, systems of great complexity and potential can be created. Such systems can be constructed on demand for specific projects but are also available as ready-made products.

Surface effects

Last but not least in the field of new materials is the subject of ornament and surface effects. Modernist architecture banished ornament and surface treatment in an attempt to make the surface express and present the structure of the building. Today this approach is in many cases no longer valid. Most façade systems today require the presence of a continuous external surface more or less independent from the building structure. Most cladding systems produce surfaces unrelated to the internal structure of the building. From the rectangular aluminum panels of the 80s to today's rain screens, metal meshes and high-pressure laminates there have been many changes and it is now possible to find a great variety of colors, textures and effects.

Digital fabrication techniques have made possible the production for the market of non-repetitive decorative patterns. Many companies offer the possibility for architects to create panels and surfaces with their own custom designs. Printing techniques have also advanced greatly and laminated panels with high-quality prints are now widely used.

Wood & plant products

Characteristics of wood species used in construction

Botanical Name	Common Name	Density (kg/m^3)	Uses
Abies albá	Fir	400	interiors, furniture, laminated wood
Acer pseudoplatanus	European Maple	640	interiors, furniture, floors
Acer saccharinum	American Maple	630-700	industrial floors, furniture
Betula alba	European Birch	640-670	structural plywood, high quality woodwork, furniture
Betula alleghaniensis	American Birch	570-710	plywood, high quality woodwork, furniture, floors
Castanea sativa	Sweet Chestnut	540-650	doors, windows, floors
Fagus sylvatica	Beech	690-750	interiors, floors, curved wooden furniture
Fraxinus americana	American Ash	560-660	plywood, cabinetmaking
Fraxinus excelsior	European Ash	680-750	floors
Juglans nigra	American Walnut	550-660	interiors, floors, plywood, furniture
Juglans regia	European Walnut	630-680	interiors, floors, plywood, furniture, only for interiors
Picea ables	Norway Spruce	440-470	framework, interiors, furniture, laminated wood
Pinus sylvestris	Scots Pine	500-540	framework, interiors, exteriors, furniture, laminated wood
Pseudotsuga menziessli	Douglas Fir	470-520	framework, exteriors, interiors, floors, plywood
Quercus alba	American White Oak	670-770	framework, interiors, floors, furniture
Quercus robur	European Oak	670-760	framework, interiors, floors, furniture
Quercus rubra	American Red Oak	650-790	interiors, floors, plywood. furniture

Antiques

Ebony and Co

Reclaimed wood from old buildings

The Antique series of products from Ebony and Co consists of woods of special character and properties that have been reclaimed from old buildings. Several species are available, each one with its own story.

The White Oak comes from the old barns of the eastern shore of the United States. For over two centuries, the timbers used to build these barns have been maturing to perfection. These beautiful old structures were made from a mixture of Red Oak and White Oak, the latter predominating. These ancient boards tell their own story of the early settlers of former colonial America, through their unique nail holes, cracks, watermarks, saw marks and other characteristics, etched by many years of faithful service.

North American Chestnut was struck by a deadly tree fungus in 1904, that wiped out the entire species. This precious product exists today only as a limited supply of carefully sourced reclaimed wood, greatly enhanced through decades of ageing. Antique Chestnut is characterised by a very deep swirled grain, creating an almost three dimensional appearance.

1

2

3

4

5

Ebony and Co
156 Fifth Ave
Suite 707
New York, NY 10010
USA

www.ebonyandco.com
Tel: +1 646-786-0330
Fax: +1 646-786-0334
E-mail: newyork@ebonyandco.com

Ebony and Co
15 Savile Row
Mayfair
London W1S 3PJUSA
UK

www.ebonyandco.com
Tel: +44 (0)2077-340-734
Fax: +44 (0)2077-340-736
E-mail: london@ebonyandco.com

6

7

1. Tommy Hilfiger Flagship store (London) - Antique Oak.
2. Antique Oak with Whitewash - Herringbone Parquet.
3. Oiled Heart Pine.
4. Unmilled Barnwood.
5. Antique Chestnut.
6. Private residence, The Hampton's (New York) - Antique Oak Whitewash Oiled.
7. Design Study (Amsterdam) - Unmilled Barnwood.

Ebony and Co
Paseo de Gracia 118, Principal
Barcelona 08008
Spain

www.ebonyandco.com
Tel: +34 902-20-3061
Fax: +34 902-20-3062
E-mail: barcelona@ebonyandco.com

Ebony and Co
Herengracht 516
1017CC
Amsterdam
The Netherlands

www.ebonyandco.com
Tel: +31 (0) 20-616-3444
Fax: +31 (0) 20-412-1777
E-mail: amsterdam@ebonyandco.com

Iconic Panels

B&N

Formed laminate with carved wood core

Iconic Panels are created using an innovative process of formed laminate over a carved wood core. Incredibly durable, they can be sawn, nailed, screwed, glued, or simply mounted on walls with B&N's special Panel Cleats.

Iconic Panels are also available with LEED-qualified, fire-rated, or water-resistant cores.

1. Iconic Versailles in Paintable Lam with latex paint.

2. Iconic Seapod in Maple.

3. Iconic Helsinki Panels in Tan Color-Core and White Matte.

4. Iconic Helvetica in Paintable Lam with latex paint.

1

2

3

B&N Industries
1409 Chapin Avenue, 2nd Floor
Burlingame, California 94010
USA

www.bnind.com
Tel: +1 650-593-4127
Fax: +35 650-593-3112
E-mail: Mail@BNind.com

4

Reclaimed Wood Iconic Panels

B&N

Decorative panels from reclaimed wood

This is a special version of Iconic Panels created from reclaimed woods. This initial collection includes three species: Western Redwood (revitalized from olive barrel staves), Douglas Fir (recycled from old gym (bleachers), and Asian Teak (procured from beautiful, yet blighted structures throughout Southeast Asia).

Beyond the unparalleled patina of the aged wood and the hard, straight grains, reclaimed timber helps us re-use and recycle materials that would otherwise become landfill.

The reclaimed timber veneer and panel substrate are both FSC (Forest Stewardship Council) certified. The finish is a low- V.O.C. varnish.

1. Carnaby Iconic Panel in Reclaimed Douglas Fir.
2. Albert Iconic Panel in Reclaimed Asian Teak.
3. Wright Iconic Panel in Reclaimed Douglas Fir.
4. Broadcast Iconic Panel in Reclaimed Douglas Fir.
5. Hitchcock Iconic Panel in Reclaimed Western Redwood.

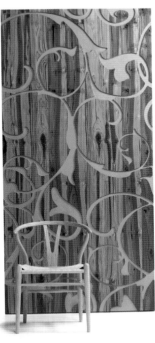

1   2   3

B&N Industries
1409 Chapin Avenue, 2nd Floor
Burlingame, California 94010
USA

www.bnind.com
Tel: +1 650-593-4127
Fax: +35 650-593-3112
E-mail: Mail@BNind.com

4

5

Suitable for outside applications and considered a good choice in the building market, MEG, the self-supporting high pressure laminate (HPL), is a long-lasting, fade resistant and weather-proof material with high technical performances. One or both sides can be decorated and it is available in any décor thanks to the digital print technique.

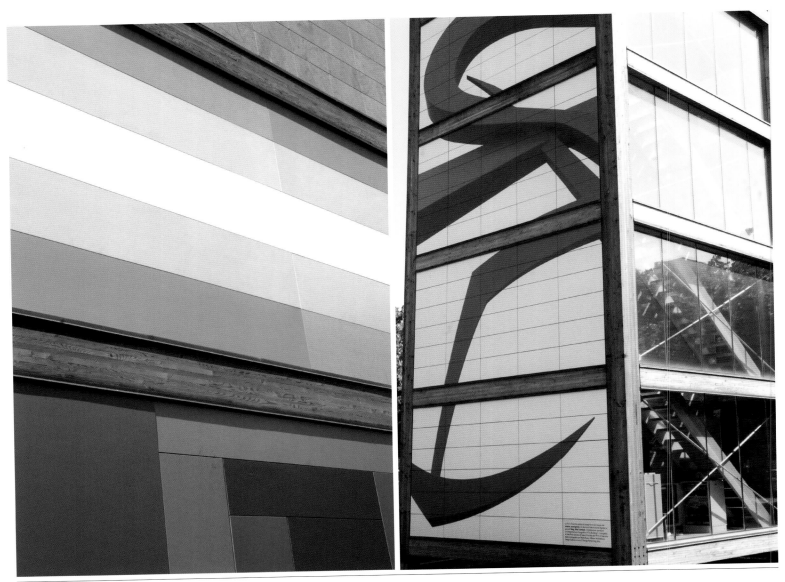

Abet Laminati S.p.A.
Viale Industria, 21 - Casella Postale 47
12042 BRA (CN)
Italy

www.abet-laminati.it
Tel: +39 0172 419111
Fax: +39 0172 431571
E-mail: abet@abet-laminati.it

Ply Wall Elements are wooden interior panels for walls and ceilings. By combining these elements continuous surfaces can be created.

Elements are made of birch plywood and solid wood frames. There are three different models: Ply 1, Ply 2 and Ply Strong.

Standard Ply-elements are available in lacquered birch, colored dark grey or cool white. The size of one element is 595 × 595 mm.

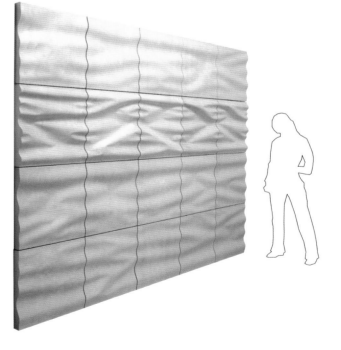

Jouko Kärkkäinen
Albertinkatu 46 B 26 B
00180 Helsinki
Finland

www.joukokarkkainen.com
Tel: +35 840-515-0008
E-mail: info@joukokarkkainen.com

Collection Digitalia

Abet Laminati - Karim Rashid

Digitally printed laminates

Designed by Karim Rashid for Abet Laminati, Collection Digitalia is the new series of 27 bright, colourful and involving decorations in digital print that seem to produce optical illusions. With the new collection for Abet Laminati Karim Rashid provides contemporary people with strong impressions, shapes and colours thus describing his philosophy: to arouse feelings and emotions.

Rashid said about the collection: *"New decorative meanings have surfaced. Once decoration spoke of ritual, religious iconography, or spiritual images - now I am interested in it speaking to us about our new spiritualism the spirit of the digital age. Decoration needs a revisit in our product and architectural landscape to communicate our milieu, our time."*

1. Aquatik.
2. Blobulous Black.
3. Installation with Collection Digitalia panels

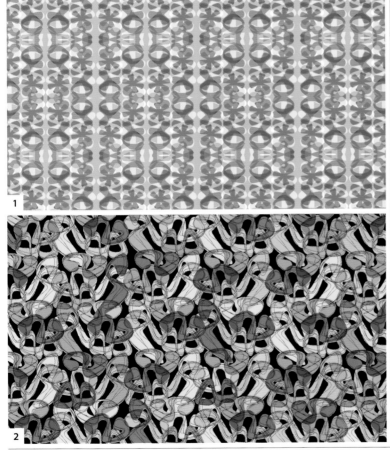

Abet Laminati S.p.A.
Viale Industria, 21 - Casella Postale 47
12042 BRA (CN)
Italy

www.abet-laminati.it
Tel: +39 0172 419111
Fax: +39 0172 431571
E-mail: abet@abet-laminati.it

Valchromat

Investwood

Throughout colored wood fibre panel

Valchromat is a wood fibre panel colored throughout with organic dyes. It has been conceived to accept all kinds of finishing (varnish, wax, oil) but can also be used in its natural state. It is available in sheets of four different sizes, in 8 colors (blue, red, grey, orange, black, green, yellow and brown) and 7 thicknesses: 8, 12, 16, 19, 22, 25 and 30mm.

It has advantages to both manufacturers and specifiers. It is easier to work with, avoids several operations during manufacture (less sanding, no painting, longer tool life, no edge banding) while being an innovative natural looking, but aesthetically flexible product. It has applications in interior decoration, furniture building, wall paneling, flooring, shop fitting, doors, kitchens, signs…

1

2

3

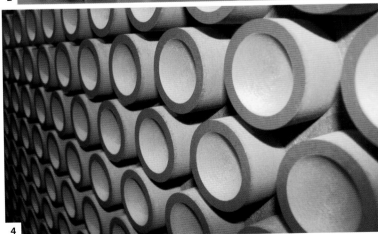

4

5

Investwood
Apartado 078
Tomar
2304-909 Valbom
Portugal

www.investwood.pt
Tel: +35 124-932-9905
Fax: +35 124-932-9915
E-mail: info@investwood.pt

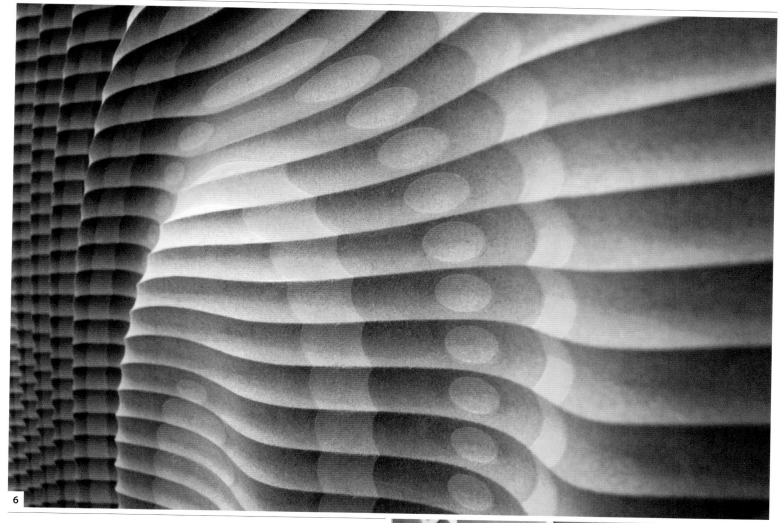

6

1. Detail of a column wrapped in Valchromat puzzled together. Made by DÉTÉ, Luxembourg.
2. Door manufactured by Dibidoku.
3. Kitchen in Switzerland made by Eskiss.
4. Close up of machined Valchromat used as wall paneling (orange over grey) – made by Interlam.
5. Table made for dVb clothing brand present in Harrods of London.
6. Close up of machined Valchromat used as wall paneling (4 layers of 8 mm red and blue) made by Interlam.
7. Wall paneling – metal laminate over orange Valchromat.

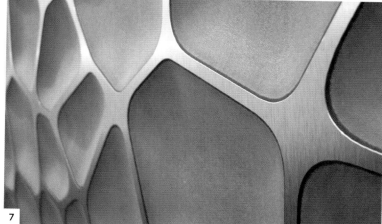

7

Duralmond

Duralmond

Panels from almond shells

Duralmond is a composite material that is obtained by mixing synthetic and natural resins, ground almond shell and other additives. After a process of polymerization and subjecting the paste to particular pressures and termperatures within a mold, this is transformed into solid finished objects, adopting from the mold forms and textures that are then applied to decorative soffits, and which sets these apart from most decorative proposals on the market. The organic redisual of the almond shell is thereby converted into a series of biodegradable and recyclable objects which by their mold fabrication can achieve diverse forms and mimick textures giving free reign to the imagination of the more adventurous designers.

Biodegradable, recyclable, light-weight, water resistant (ideal for humid areas), with good acoustic properties, and suitable performance against fire, Duralmond is the ideal material for interior design and decoration.

1

2

3

Revestimientos y Techos Duralmond
Avda. Región Murciana, Parcela ITC-2/3
Pol. Ind. Base 2000
30564 Lorquí. Murcia
Spain

www.duralmond.com
Tel: +34 (9)6-869-4453
Fax: +34 (9)6-869-4524
E-mail: duralmond@duralmond.com

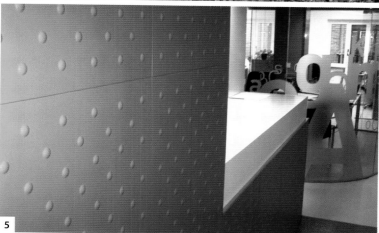

1. Nipon: a square based tile with a raised spherical section.
2. Cuttos: a square based tile with a slight curve along all four edges giving a central plane that occupies most of the surface, looking like padding.
3. Chapas: a rectangular based tile with simulated rivets round the edge.
4. Paperwall: the piece simulates two separated and slightly disorganised piles of paper. The mimetic quality of the material gives this a surprising effect.
5. Golfin: a square based tile with small semi-spheres arranged regularly over the surface.

Timbercrete

Timbercrete Pty Ltd Australia

Recycled timber waste as sustainable building material

Timbercrete blocks, bricks, panels and pavers are made of recycled sawmill waste, sand and cement. Its main ingredient is recycled timber waste. The bricks and blocks are produced in a mould at normal temperatures and they have an insulation value over 4 times better than normal bricks.

It has the highest possible fire resistance rating for building materials. It is impervious to rot, termites, and is even bullet-proof. The longevity is the same as other concrete products (hundreds of years) and easily withstands the extremes of the weather, hot, wet, freezing and rapid freeze-thaw cycles.

The colour is apricot-yellow in Australia, due to the colour of the sand used, but can be any, by using other sand or adding a coulorant. Timbercrete bricks and blocks can be made in any size, shape or texture by using the proper mould.

Its density is less or the same as water, so the bricks and blocks are typically larger although not heavy, and easy to lay. This reduces costs and increases the speed of construction. It is made of relatively cheap raw materials and has low energy consumption during production and transport. And it is easy to use because it can be nailed and screwed into, like timber.

Timbercrate
2627 Bells Line of Rd
Bilpin, NSW, 2758
Australia

www.timbercrete.com.au
Tel: +61 24-567-1149
Fax: +61 24-567-1150
E-mail: peter@timbercrete.com.au

The approach of Baubotanik is to understand architecture as an aspect of botany by using growing wooden plants in construction. Baubotanik attempts to combine the aesthetic qualities of growing trees with the requirements of structural statics and principles of engineering.

Baubotanik uses two phenomenons of tree growth. The ability of trees, to grow together, and their ability, to swell over external materials.

By interconnecting plants with technical elements, the whole structure merges to a hybrid composite, which can be used as a load bearing system.

Systems like this develop their own characters and particularities. Aesthetic qualities are immediately developed by the partly autonomous growth of the plants, and the future shape is dominated by the imbruting of the shoot in summer, while in winter, the construction is barely visible.

While the slowly increasing stability is reliant on the natural growth speed, the architect accelerates the basic development of a full-grown tree, by constructing it artificially e.g. in the form of trussed girders.

Baubotanik, Research and Development
Innerer Nordbahnhof 1
D-70191 Stuttgart
Germany

www.baubotanik.com
Tel: +49 (0) 711-933-5770
E-mail: info@baubotanik.de

PureBond

Columbia Forest Products

Formaldehyde-free hardwood plywood

The original cost-competitive decorative hardwood plywood without the formaldehyde. PureBond® is Columbia Forest Products' exclusive formaldehyde-free innovation for hardwood plywood manufacturing.

Replacing traditional urea formaldehyde (uf) hardwood plywood construction with non-toxic, soy-based PureBond technology enables Columbia to eliminate any added formaldehyde from standard veneer-core and non-UF composite hardwood plywood core panels.

What makes PureBond plywood special is that it is cost-competitive with the standard uf construction of most decorative veneer-core hardwood plywood that is made today. That means PureBond is substantially less expensive than other no-added-formaldehyde alternatives currently available.

Additionally, PureBond is even more water resistant than uf panels– approaching the requirements for Type I, or waterproof performance. PureBond formaldehyde-free panels have out-performed uf bonded panels in all moisture degradation tests.

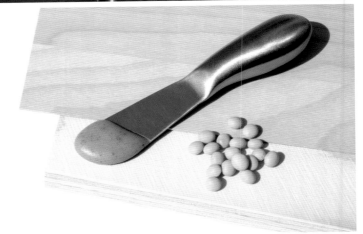

Columbia Forest Products
7820 Thorndike Road
Greensboro, NC 27409
USA

www.choosecolumbia.com
Tel: +1 800-637-1609

Columbia Forest Products has partnered with Teragren to offer the best of both worlds: Teragren bamboo face veneers and PureBond® formaldehyde-free veneer core hardwood plywood technology. Available in four popular styles of vertical and flat grain bamboo veneers in natural and caramelized colorations to complement any décor. And because they are harvested from rapidly renewable bamboo and feature PureBond technology, users are guaranteed that these panels are friendly to the natural and interior environments.

Columbia and Teragren bamboo panels on veneer core contribute to LEED® EQ Credit 4.4 for Low Emitting Materials because they are made with PureBond formaldehyde-free technology. They also contribute to the LEED® MR Credit 6 for Rapidly Renewable Materials because they are made with Optimum 5.5 Moso Bamboo, a rapidly renewable resource.

Columbia Forest Products
7820 Thorndike Road
Greensboro, NC 27409
USA

www.choosecolumbia.com
Tel: +1 800-637-1609

Obersound

Oberflex - 5.5 designers

Textured acoustic panels

Oberflex has decided to work with the 5.5 designers agency to conduct research into its Obersound panels, and to deliver a new collection of panels liable to offer an entirely new response to architects and designers. The 5.5 designers have given priority to redefine the visual possibilities of the panels according to new technical possibilities. They have devised an idea according to which the panel is dealt with like textile or wallpaper.

The 5.5 designers have come up with an idea of perforations that suggest climate, skin, textile, vegetation or even sound waves to elaborate the new Obersound collection. The acoustic panels become a decorative component in their own right. Beyond its technical qualities, it finds a new graphic identity that enriches the environment in which it is used. With the new Obersound panels, the acoustic panel becomes a support to the imagination in the service of creation and the architectural environment.

OBER SA
Longeville en Barrois
55014 Bar Le Duc Cedex
France

www.oberflex.fr
Tel: +33 (0)32-976-7778
Fax: +33 (0)32-945-37 37
E-mail: obercom@oberflex.fr

The core range is the Oberflex® real wood veneer high-pressure laminate, which offers the best of both worlds: the aesthetics and warmth of real wood in more than 30 wood species, and the surface resistance and longevity of HPL. Installation and maintenance are also as easy as for any HPL. It finds applications in most prestigious public spaces, from the floor to the ceiling, not forgetting walls and furniture – this is why we call it the « ystème Bois®» (the "Wood System").

Oberflex® is available in five surface finishes:

Satin: looks and feels like waxed wood

Relief: highlights the genuine relief of the wood grain

Matt: enhances the natural look of the veneer

Brushed: combines the natural look of the Matt effect with the feel of raw wood

Pearlescent: blend of silk & metal effect

Additional trendy collections have been added to the original Oberflex® real wood veneer laminate line:

Les Sablés by Oberflex: sandblasted real wood veneer laminate

Spiced Wood Collection: linear contrasts between the tint and the colour of the wood

Textured Wood Collection : nuances of white, black and grey combined with 6 different patterns

Natural shades : unique process adapted from 3 different patterns and combined with veneer species – striking shadows and colour contrasts

Ober SA
Longeville en Barrois
55014 Bar Le Duc Cedex
France

www.oberflex.fr
Tel: +33 (0)32-976-7778
Fax: +33 (0)32-945-37 37
E-mail: obercom@oberflex.fr

Abaca, Buntal, Piña

Windochine

Hand-loomed fabrics comprised of natural fibers

Windochine designs and produces one-of-a-kind hand loomed fabrics comprised of natural fibers from a wide variety of bamboo and grasses native to Southeast Asia and China, including abaca, raffia, buntal palm, bacbac bark, hemp, jute, and pineapple fiber. Abaca, also called Manila Hemp, is a close relative of the banana. Drawn from the inner part of the abaca tree, it is renowned for its high tensile strength and durability. Prior to weaving, abaca fiber is beaten rhythmically by hand using traditional paddles for softening and to release the natural cellulose, resulting in a high silky luster and smooth, cool finish. Certain Windochine designs incorporate other useful parts of the abaca tree, such as bacbac, its bark-like dried outer leaf sheath.

Among Windochine's most elegant and refined textiles are those woven of pineapple fiber, or Piña, a strong white or creamy cobweb-like fiber drawn from the tall leaves of an indigenous wild pineapple plant. The fiber is hand stripped from the leaves, sunbleached, hand knotted and spun. As piña fiber recovery is only about 1%, it can take six months to gather enough fiber to produce two pounds of spun piña.

Resembling a very fine, polished bamboo, Buntal is a thin cylindrical filament drawn from the leaf-stalk of the Buri (raffia) palm. Woven buntal creates a two-dimensional fabric of polished finish and geometric refinement.

1

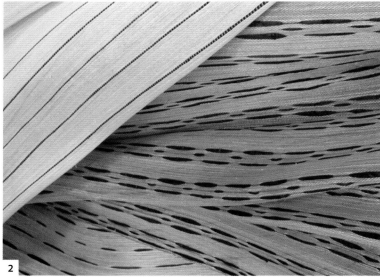

2

3

Windochine USA
1371 El Corto Drive
Altadena, CA 91001
USA

www.windochine.com
Tel: +1 626-798-8485
Fax: +1 323-576-5337
E-mail: info@windochine.com

1. Abaca hanging panels
2. Abaca
3. Buntal
4. Pina
5. Pina bed drapery
6. Weaving of Buntal
7. Buntal

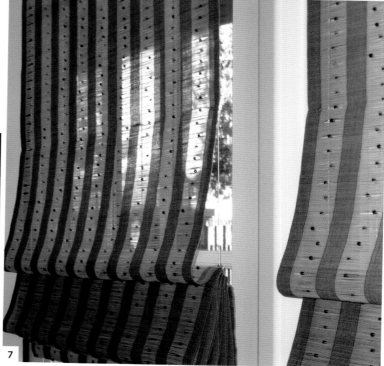

Barskin

Caba Co.

Hand-made surface covering from tree bark

Barskin™ is a natural, hand made wood material that is acid free and created with an environmentally sustainable process that dates from pre-Columbian times. The bark is processed with cold and then boiling water, hand pounded and sun dried. The resulting Barskin has a variety of beautiful tones and textures, in several natural, hybrid and designer colors, bringing a sense of stone, parchment or leather to a variety of applications. The dramatic beauty of Barskin embodies the authentic textures, tones and nuances exclusive to natural materials.

Barskin can be used for wall covering, ceiling covering, furniture surfaces, lampshades, as well as a variety of other applications. Homes, offices, retail and hospitality environments are all enhanced by its unique character.

Barskin can be easily manipulated, applied and sealed for protection, all with environmentally friendly techniques.

1

2

1. Multi-color Barskin wall, Palomino Barksin table surface & lampshade
2. Palomino Barskin wallcovering, Brownstone Furniture Showroom, San Francisco.
3. Ivory & Palomino Barskin
4. Barskin Naturals collection
5. Contemporary Barskin - shown in Gray
6. Woven Ivory Barskin

Caba Company
1310 Don Gaspar
Santa Fe NM, 87505
USA

www.barkskin.com
Tel: +1 505-983-1942
Fax: +1 505-988-7183
E-mail: caba@barkskin.com

DalNaturel

Dalsouple

Natural rubber flooring

DalNaturel is a new generation natural rubber floor covering that boasts exceptional environmental credentials yet demands no compromise on colour, design or performance. Manufactured to the same exacting performance standards as Dalsouple's standard synthetic rubber products, and available in virtually all of the 80 gorgeous colours and 30 textures in the Dalsouple range, DalNaturel comprises over 90 % natural ingredients.

Natural rubber is a wholly renewable raw material, and rubber trees are exceptionally efficient at carbon sequestration – the absorption of harmful CO_2 from the atmosphere. So for every square metre of DalNaturel produced, over 7 kilos of carbon dioxide are absorbed by the mature rubber trees used to make it. This is around 7 times more efficient than linoleum, which is made from linseed plants, while PVC, as a synthetic material, achieves zero carbon sequestration.

Manufacturing energy for rubber flooring is extremely low in comparison to other resilient floor products. Rubber is also easy to recycle, not just once but several times, with many potential applications. All these factors, combined with an energy efficient production process and long service life, contribute to an environmental life cycle performance that is worlds away from existing products.

DalNaturel natural rubber is beautiful, tactile, flexible, warm and soft. In addition to our standard ranges most products are available in an infinite palette of richly saturated custom colours made to customer specification. It has many other benefits that make it suitable for a wide range of applications. It insulates, absorbs impact and noise and resists both water and burns. It is slip resistant, supple, tough, practical and hygienic.

1

1. Anglia Ruskin University Library. Designed by Curious Group.
2. Selection of textured designs.
3. Selection of colours.

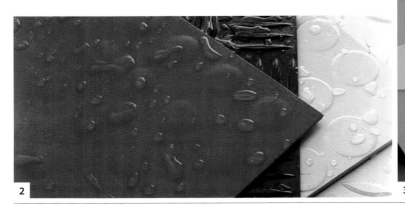

2

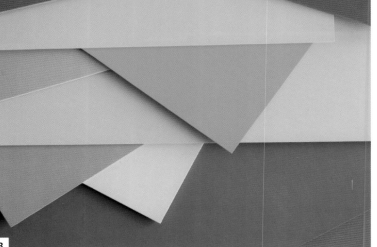

3

Dalsouple
Showground Road
Bridgwater
Somerset, TA6 6AJ
England

www.dalsouple.com
Tel: +44 (0)127-872-7777
Fax: +44 (0)127-872-7788
E-mail: info@dalsouple.com

ModuTile modular flooring is a versatile way to customize and re-define space on a budget. Made from cork, ModuTiles feel good on your feet and tread lightly on the planet.

Create rugs, runners or cover entire floors with the texture and warmth of cork ModuTiles. Each set of six tan, and six chocolate cork shaped tiles covers 12 square feet and comes with peel and stick adhesive tabs for temporary installation. Rotate tiles to configure fun and flexible patterns and cover old, chipped or stained ceramic, linoleum, concrete or wood for a fresh look. Replace modules as needed or install them permanently with standard cork flooring adhesives and finishes. Coat them with waxes, oils or stains for color and greater durability.

MIO
446 North 12th Street
Philadelphia, PA 19123
USA

www.mioculture.com
Tel: +1 215-925-9359
E-mail: info@mioculture.com

MIO
Aegidienberger Str. 18
D-50939 Koeln
Germany

www.mioculture.com
Tel: +49 221-168-31193
E-mail: europe@mioculture.com

Fortis Arbor

Flux Studios

Wood tile mosaics

Fortis Arbor wood tile mosaics are handcrafted from solid bamboo, teak and rosewood. By partnering with a small furniture company the company reclaim rosewood and teak from sustainably harvested and plantation grown lumber too small to be used in furniture making. All tiles have a living finish that is easily maintained and enhances the wood's natural beauty. Each tile is cut and finished by hand, so every installation is unique.

Fortis Arbor Mosaics can be used in virtually any interior application with limited water exposure: on walls, back splashes, countertops, fireplace surrounds and kitchen, bathroom and high traffic floors. Whether the tiles are used in a contemporary or traditional setting, Fortis Arbor Mosaics bring a depth and aesthetic harmony to the environment that is unrivaled by other materials.

Fortis Arbor Grout - patent pending - was developed specifically to move with the natural expansion and contraction of Fortis Arbor wood tiles. Flux Studios are the pioneers of wood tile mosaics and the company's grout allows for maximum performance and easy installation.

Flux Studios, Inc.
4001 North Ravenswood Ave
Unit 603
Chicago, Illinois 60613
USA

www.fluxstudios.com
Tel: +1 773-883-2030
E-mail: fluxstudios@sbcglobal.net

Vinterio Nimbus combines various wood species for unlimited design potential. Surface patterns can be wild and expressive, classically elegant or exclusively unique. Customers can use Vinterio Nimbus to create individual and exclusive designs which are totally different from conventional wooden surfaces.

Vinterio Nimbus opens up a number of high-quality surfaces which combine various wood species. Surface patterns can be wild and expressive, classically elegant or exclusively unique. Architects and designers can create their own real wooden pattern according to their ideas and needs. Vinterio also holds several Standard Nimbus patterns in stock. Vinterio Nimbus is an exclusive and unique product with a variable component width of 6 – 25 mm. It is well-suited for architectural and design minded applications, furniture, doors, kitchen cabinets, decorative panels, wrappings, moldings, flooring and the marine industry.

All processes comply with the highest standards. Strict quality demands on the raw material ensure a balanced and high-quality appearance. Surface patterns can always be repeated in exact detail, thanks to the new component design and innovative manufacturing process developed by Danzer Group. At the same time, each Vinterio surface maintains its individual specie characteristics.

Vinterio AG
Schutzengelstrasse 36
Postfach 2461
6342 Baar
Switzerland

www.vinterio.com
Tel: +41 41-560-7860
Fax: +41 41-560-7861

Albeflex Veneer

Albeflex

Flexible wood veneer

Albeflex offers a series of products based on a technology for creating flexible wood veneers. This is a sheet of sliced veneer that has been bonded to a paper backing which prevents any glue used in applying the veneer to its substrate from leaking through. This is a highly flexible veneered sheet that is no longer prone to splitting, unlike most veneers, so that it can be bent and moulded. It can also be rolled up which greatly improves storage and transportation. The Albeflex veneer has many benefits: It is hight pliable and can bend in both directions up to a radius of 3 mm; it is easy to apply with all types of adhesive; it can be cut even with simple scissors or a cutter; and it can be made from all wood types.

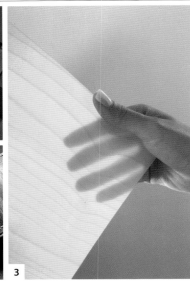

1. Light made from Albeflex Lightwood.
2. Sewn veneer. Albeflex veneer can be aplied to suport materials that allow sewing.
3. Albeflex Lightwood. Semi-transparent veneer that can be used for lighting.
4. Section of Albeflex Softwood.
5. Albeflex Softwood. Veneer-covered foam, flexible and with acoustic qualities, that can be used in furniture.
6. KL veneer sheet.

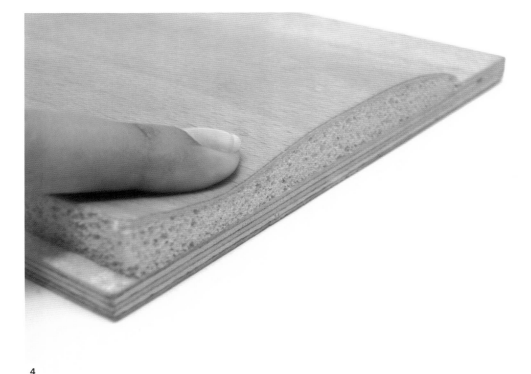

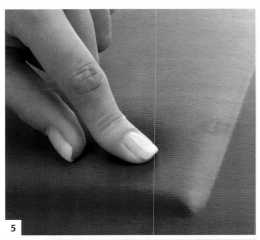

Albeflex slr
1a Strada delle Paludi
Francenigo,
31010 Gaiarine (TV)
Italy

www.albeflex.it
Tel: +39 043-476-8492
Fax: +39 043-476-7752
E-mail: info@albeflex.it

Nendo designed the cabbage chair for the 21st Century Man exhibition curated by Issey Miyake. Miyake asked nendo to make furniture out of the pleated paper that is produced in bulk during the process of making pleated fabric, and usually abandoned as an unwanted by-product. The solution to this challenge was to trasform a roll of pleated paper into a small chair that appears naturally as you peel away its outside layers, one layer at a time.

Resins added during the original paper production process add strength and the ability to remember forms, and the pleats themselves give the chair elasticity and a springy resilience, for an overall effect that looks almost rough, but gives the user a soft, comfortable seating experience.

Since the production process is so simple, the chair could be shipped as one compact roll for the user to cut open and peel back at home. The chair has no internal structure and it is assembled without nails or screws. This primitive design responds gently to fabrication and distribution costs and environmental concerns, the kinds of issues that we face in the 21st century.

Nendo

2-2-16-5F Shimomeguro Meguro-ku
Tokyo 153-0064
Japan

www.nendo.jp
Tel: +81 (0) 36-661-3750
Fax: +81 (0) 36-661-3751
E-mail: info@nendo.jp

This line of modular PaperForms constitutes a practical and affordable solution for transforming light to medium traffic environments. Tile rotation creates an infinite variety of patterns putting users in control of the design. Whether covering entire rooms, a single wall or applied as part of the decor, the modular tiles grow with the space. Made from 100% post and pre-consumer waste paper, PaperForms are the smarter and more environmentally sound choice.

The tiles can be used in a section or an entire room to great effect. Replacing individual tiles when needed is simple. Mixing and matching patterns affords unlimited freedom. Going modular means using less and only where it's needed, providing texture and color the smart way.

All tiles are made from 100% post and pre-consumer waste paper. Percentage of pre and post-consumer paper varies depends on the final color of the product. PaperForms in colors are generally 100% pre-consumer waste paper unless otherwise specified. All materials are sourced locally at each of the production facilities in order to minimize energy consumption. Special colors and types of paper or pulp can be specified for custom projects.

MIO
446 North 12th Street
Philadelphia, PA 19123
USA

www.mioculture.com
Tel: +1 215-925-9359
E-mail: info@mioculture.com

MIO
Aegidienberger Str. 18
D-50939 Koeln
Germany

www.mioculture.com
Tel: +49 221-168-31193
E-mail: europe@mioculture.com

Wellboard

Well

Profiled board from 100% cellulose

Wellboard consists of 100% cellulose with no added adhesives or binders. The different profiles are pressed into the flat base plate using heat and pressure. In spite of its high stability, wellboard is a lightweight material: the different types weigh between 1.25 And 2.7 Kg/m².

The material is available in six different profile types. Wellboard minimum, medium and maximum as well as wellboard alpha 800 have a corrugated profile. They differ in the height and width of the corrugations and in the thickness of the panels. Wellboard gamma 300 and gamma 500 have a trapeze-shaped profile. As a result of their design, they have flat supporting surfaces which make it easier to glue and screw them to carrier materials and to attach mounting and fixing elements.

Wellboard's corrugated surface and flexibility make it an excellent material for exhibition, shop and furniture construction. Regardless of whether it's used for the counter or the back wall of the booth, a roll-front cupboard or a screen – wellboard gives the objects an unmistakable face.

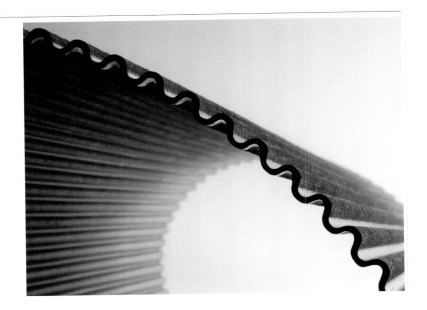

Well Ausstellungssystem gmbh
Schwarzer Bär 2
30449 Hannover
Germany

www.well.de
Tel: +49 511-928-8110

Made from recycled, double-wall cardboard, Nomad is a modular architectural system that can be assembled into free-standing, sculptural screens, temporary partitions, rooms or even displays without hardware, tools or damage to existing structures. Available in nine colors, Nomad can be arranged into open or closed configurations; creating private environments or light and airy dividers. The Nomad system can be configured to create entry-ways and corners, easily adjusting to any indoor space.

Nomadic lifestyles and the desire for flexible space inspired the creation of Nomad. Designed to grow and adapt to any environment and a range of applications, Nomad Architectural System translates the tools of architecture into simple modules that anyone can use.

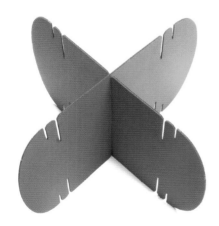

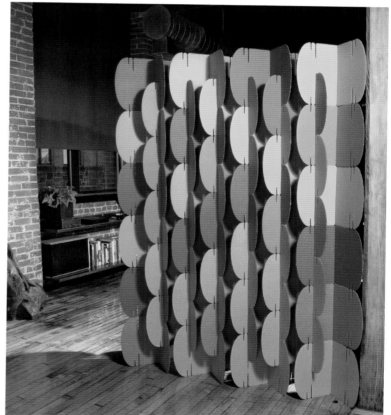

MIO
446 North 12th Street
Philadelphia, PA 19123
USA

www.mioculture.com
Tel: +1 215-925-9359
E-mail: info@mioculture.com

MIO
Aegidienberger Str. 18
D-50939 Koeln
Germany

www.mioculture.com
Tel: +49 221-168-31193
E-mail: europe@mioculture.com

Types of cement and their components in proportion to mass

Type	Designation	Clínker	Steel Slag (S)	Natural Pozzolan (Z)	Fly Ash (C)	Limestone Filler (F)	Additional Components
Portland Cements	I-0	100	0	0	0	0	0
	I	95 - 99	—	—	—	—	1 - 5
White Portland Cements	I-B	95 - 100	—	—	—	—	0 - 5
Composite Portland Cement	II	65 - 88	6 - 27	6 - 23		0 - 5	—
Portland Cement with Slag	II-S	65 - 94	6 - 35	—	—	—	0 - 5
Portland Pozzolan Cement	II-Z	72 - 94	—	6 - 28	—	—	0 - 5
Portland Flyash Cement	II-C	72 - 94	—	—	6 - 28	—	0 - 5
Portland Cement with limestone filler	II-F	80 - 94	—	—	—	6 - 15	0 - 5
White Blended Portland Cements	II-B	75 - 94	—	—	—	—	6-25
Blastfurnace Cements	III-1	40 - 64	36 - 60	—	—	—	0 - 5
	III-2	20 - 39	61 - 80	—	—	—	0 - 5
Pozzolanic Cement	IV	- 60	—	< 40		—	0 - 5
Blended Cement	V	20 - 64		36 - 80		—	0 - 5
White Cements for floors	V-B	40-70	—	—	—	—	30-60
Aluminate Cement	VI	100	—	—	—	—	—

fibre C

Rieder

Concrete panels with glassfibre reinforcement

FibreC is an innovative concrete panel strengthend by glassfibre components. The material provides an ideal solution for modern architecture and interior design.

Concrete is one of the most frequently used building nevertheless still has enormous unutilized innovative potential. Firstly concrete as an authentic building material corresponds to the latest trend for the use of natural, environment-friendly and economic building materials while still being capable of producing modern finishes.

Due to the extreme durability and robust character concrete resists high pressures with maximum panel size at minimum thickness. Available standard measures for fibreC panels are 1.20 x 3.60 m but can be stretched to a length of 5.00 m with a minimum thickness of 13 mm. The material has excellent thermal resistance for absolute safety in terms of temperature stability (standing up to 350°) and therefore provides optimum fire protection for multi-storey buildings up to a height of 100 m. The unique characteristics additionally provide protection against vandalism which is a central decision criterion for material choice especially in the public domain.

FibreC is high-strength, thin, flexible and malleable and can be used in special forms flat as well as rounded. Rough edges as well as roundings and curves can be achieved within a single flowing material without adhesives. It has high durability and breaks the limits for traditional architecture and interior design. Various visual effects can be achieved by using covered or uncovered fixing solutions.

Another dimension for playing with the endless varieties marks the possibilities for color selection and defining of different surface structures. The color palette ranges from any grayscale tone to natural tones such as teracotta, green or brown. Different structures, matt polished or brushed emphasizes the modern face of glass fibre concrete. The characteristics are particlarly evident in interior design. Genuine natural stone mixed with ferric oxide colors creates a perfect color finish and without applying a coating "Technical Marble" evolves over time.

1

2

1. Opera House Bregenz. Architects: Dietrich/Untertrifaller.
2. National Park Center, Mittersill, Austria. Architects: Forsthuber & Scheithauer
3. FSI Frank Stronach Institute Graz. Zinterl Architects ZT.
4. Railway Station Vienna North. Architect: Wimmer.
5. SPA VW Wolfsburg, Germany. Architect: Wehberg.

Rieder Faserbeton-Elemente GmbH   **www.rieder.cc**
Glasberg 1   Tel.: +49 (0) 803-190-1670
83059 Kolbermoor   Fax: +49 / (0)80-319-0167-169
Germany   E-mail: office@rieder.cc

3

4

5

Ductal

Lafarge

Fiber-reinforced ductile concrete

This fiber-reinforced, ultra-high performance material combines strength with casting fluidity, facilitating the creation of highly complex and elegantly simple forms.

Ductal® can be a preferred alternative to steel, cast iron, aluminum, plastic or wood and can be used to compliment or contrast these other materials.

For the satisfaction of architects seeking to combine technological performance and aesthetics. Ductal®'s unique mechanical properties – compressive strengths (up to 200 MPa), flexural strengths (up to 40 MPa) and ductility allow for longer spans, reduced sections and volumes.

Ductal® is preferred for its resistance to corrosion, abrasion, carbonation and impact strength. It is ideal for structures built in harsh settings such as marine or industrial environments and buildings open to the public with demanding maintenance and safety requirements.

Casting ease and fluidity facilitate the construction of large-scale, highly complex, very thin precast structures that conventional concrete materials are unable to achieve. Applications including building envelopes, acoustic sound panels, facing walls, cornice outlines, flooring and other applications can be given a wide range of textures due to the materials outstanding ability to replicate mold, formwork and pattern surface detail.

1

2

1. **Helicoidal staircase build with Ductal. Architect: Cogitech.**
   Photo: Eric Bergoend. © Médiathèque Lafarge, Eric Bergoend, Cogitech, Esca Industrie, SA Escaliers Décors.
2. **Villa Navarra in Provence, France. Architect: Rudy Ricciotti.**
   Photo: Philippe Ruault. © Philippe Ruault, Rudy Ricciotti.
3. **Seonyu footbridge in Seoul, South Korea. Architect: Rudy Ricciotti.**
   Photo: E. Jae-Seong. © Médiathèque Lafarge, E. Jae-Seong, Rudy Ricciotti.
4. **The City of Calgary's Glenmore Legsby pedestrian bridge, Alberta, Canada. Architect: Evamy Cohos.**
   Photo: Tucker Photography. © Médiathèque Lafarge, Vic Tucker, Cohos Evamy, Ville de Calgary.
5. **Rehabilitation with Ductal of the main front in the swimming pool of Clichy-La-Garenne, France. Architect: ENIA Architecture.**
   Photo: Benoît Fougeirol. © Médiathèque Lafarge, Benoît Fougeirol, ENIA Architecture.
6. **The new RATP bus center in Thiais, France. Architect: Agence ECDM, Emmanuel Combarel, Dominique Marrec.**
   Photo: Benoît Fougeirol. © Médiathèque Lafarge - RATP, Benoît Fougeirol, Agence ECDM, Emmanuel Combarel, Dominique Marrec.

Lafargue
61, rue des Belles Feuilles
BP 40 - 75782 Paris Cedex 16
France

www.ductal-lafarge.com
Fax: +33 (0) 14-911-4414
E-mail: ductal@lafarge-ciments.lafarge.com

3
4
5
6

Made with nearly 70% post-industrial recycled materials, ecoX retains the verve of extremeconcrete® and adds an earth-friendly dimension. ecoX challenges the notion that recycled is somehow less than original. This ecologically sensitive material offers potential LEED credits, prevents items from filling up landfills and presents a whole much greater than the sum of its parts. And all this while providing an attractive aesthetic.

meld USA
3001-103 Spring Forest Road
Raleigh, NC 27616
USA

www.meldusa.com
Tel: +1 919-790-1749
Fax: +1 919-790-1750
E-mail: info@meldusa.com

Litracon™ is a combination of optical fibers and fine concrete. It can be produced as prefabricated building blocks and panels. Due to the small size of the fibers, they blend into concrete becoming a component of the material like small pieces of aggregate. In this manner, the result is not only two materials - glass in concrete - mixed, but a third, new material, which is homogeneous in its inner structure and on its main surfaces as well.

The glass fibers lead light by points between the two sides of the blocks. Because of their parallel position, the light-information on the brighter side of such a wall appears unchanged on the darker side. The most interesting form of this phenomenon is probably the sharp display of shadows on the opposing side of the wall. Moreover, the color of the light also remains the same.

The proportion of the fibers is very small (4%) compared to the total volume of the blocks. Moreover, these fibers mingle in the concrete because of their insignificant size, and they become a structural component as a kind of modest aggregate. Therefore, the surface of the blocks remains homogeneous concrete. In theory, a wall structure built from light-transmitting concrete can be several meters thick, because the fibers work without almost any loss in light up until 20 meters. Load-bearing structures can be also built of these blocks, since glass fibres do not have a negative effect on the well-known high compressive strength value of concrete. The blocks can be produced in various sizes and with embedded heat-isolation.

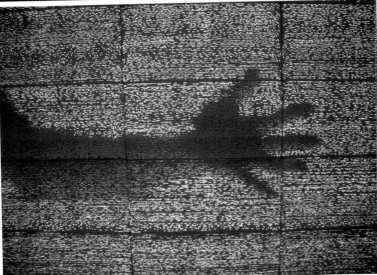

Litracon Kft.
Tanya 832
6640 Csongrád
Hungary

www.litracon.hu
Tel: +36 30-255-1648
E-mail: info@litracon.hu

Luccon Lightconcrete is a combination of modern concrete and embedded fiber optic cables. Fiber upon fiber light is projected through the construction element – for example images beyond a wall appear pointwise or digitized on the opposite side, regardless of whether they are shadows, light, colors, projections or displays. The dimensions of the construction element are basically irrelevant with one exception: With increasing thickness the experienced image on the hidden side appears increasingly peculiar and strange. Moving images are displayed in a fascinating manner and make the stone surface look iridescently lucent. The transparency of the stone lets one suspect more than is shown and suggests a curious airiness in spite of the heavy compactness.

Luccon characteristically transforms back into stone when it changes from dark to light – or when a wall wanders from day into night.

An innovative method has made it possible to produce thermally separated elements with the same transparency as the "standard" product. On both sides – outside and inside – Luccotherm shows the attractive Luccon look in spite of an insulating layer.

1. The effect of Luccon.
2. Luccon used as a bar countertop.
3. The interior of the new Luccon showroom opened in sprnig 2009 in Hagen, Germany and where all kinds of application of Luccon can be viewed.

Material Art GmbH
Elbershallen - Alte Brunnenhalle
Dödterstraße 10
D-58095 Hagen
Germany

www.luccon.com
Tel: +49 2331-340-29-40
Fax: +49 2331-340-29-41
E-mail: udo.ellerbrake@luccon.com

Panel Omega Zeta

CIRCA S.A.

Lightweight façade panel

Omega Zeta panels are produced on an industrial scale and can be customized in size, texture, color and mechanic perforations. Because of its versatility regarding its design and the properties that it presents as an effecitve thermal and acoustic insulator this is the ideal solution for modern architecture. It can be assembled three times faster thatn conventional systems, is ecological and recylcable as well as being highly resistant to weather conditions and earthquakes.

The panels for façades are composed of high resistance mortar and metal covering bidirectionally pretensed. They are highly versatile since they can be produced in size, color and finish according to the customer's wishes. The panels allow for perforations also customized in shape and size. This panel is waterproof and fire resistant.

The modular dry construction system implies the industrialization of the construction process, reducing costs and injecting flexibility into assembly. The panels are very light-weight and are 3 cm thick. The panels and the industrialized fabrication system represent a new solution, paving the way towards sustainable and innovative architecture, since they provide 50 to 80 % energy savings, are ecological and recyclable.

The industrial process, which is 95% automatic, allows the panels to be customized to suit the needs of each project regarding size and finish. This modular wall element, assemble from the exterior, comes in different sizes up to 220 × 300 cm.

CIRCA S.A.
C/ Lleida, 17 Pol. Ind. El Pla
08185 Lliçà de Vall-Barcelona
Spain

www.panelomegazeta.com
Tel: +34 902-223-800
Fax: +34 938-436-058
E-mail: comercial@panelomegazeta.com

5

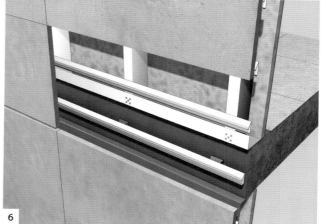

6

1. L'Ecoedifici, office building by Miquel Sitjá (La Vola).
2. Burlada Town Hall by Emilio Moncada y Carlos Iraburu.
3. Church in Miribilla by IMB Arquitectos.
4. Library of the Blanquerna University, by V.V.V.Arquitectes,SCP.
5. Single-family house in Sitges by Jon Tugores.
6. Detail of ventilated façade construction with the Omega Zeta Panel.
Photographs: Carlos Fradera Laplaza

Trend's agglomerates are made from up to 80% industrial and post-consumer recycled materials. Their value doesn't lie in their resistance, versatility and aesthetic appeal alone: used glass and production excess, destined to become waste, gives the agglomerate surfaces their shine.

The Cristallino agglomerate is made from scrap products such as washing machines doors, rearview mirrors, carlights and from recycled glass bottles and containers. It is obtained by mixing the granules of glass with a pigmented polymer which gives it its color. The transparency of the glass gives the slabs an attractive depth. Rocksolid is made from remains of quarry extractions. By combining quartz and granite in different percentages infinite combinations of colors can be obtained.

All Trend's agglomerates (Touch, Cristallino, Prezioso, Rocksolid - and TrendQ for USA) are GREENGUARD Children & Schools certified: this means that they have no dangerous volatile organic emissions (VOC) and guarantee the quality of air of indoor environments. Together with Trend's green mosaics they help achieve LEED points envisioned for sustainable buildings.

1. Cristallino. Missoni Event, Villa Alle Scalette, Vicenza, Italy.

2. Cristallino. Architectural studio, Milan, Italy.

3. Cristallino and Rocksolid. "Lexus Lifestyle Living Room" by Arcila-Duque furniture interiors, Casadecor '07 Miami, Florida, USA.

4. Cristallino. Blue Finn cafè, London, UK. 11.04 Architects Ltd - Arch. Chris Roche.

TREND GROUP S.p.A.
Piazzale Fraccon, 8
36100 Vicenza
Italy

www.trend-vi.com
Tel: +39 044-433-8711
Fax: +39 044-473-8747
E-mail: info@trend-vi.com

The use of elastic RECKLI®-Formliners for texturing the exposed face of concrete surfaces has attained a high degree of acceptance in terms of quality, ease of use and economic efficiency. The elasticity of the formliners removes the risk of damage to the hardened concrete allowing intricate detail to be used. This system has given architects, planners and designers the freedom to realize unlimited ideas in their designs for the past 35 years.

The new generation of RECKLI® Photo-Engraving Formliners expands these possibilities. The combination of the RECKLI®-System and the Photo-Engraving Technology creates a surface pattern which can vary from fine to course depending on the resolution of the image used. This image can then be incorporated onto the finished concrete surface by using the RECKLI® Formliner system.

The Photo-Engraving Process is a computer-based method for transferring image data onto sheet materials by means of milling technology. First an image template is scanned and converted into 256-grayscale. In order to transfer the image onto the sheet material, a machining file is generated from the identified grey values, whereby the file includes milling commands for a special CNC milling machine.

The milled model is used as a master for casting the elastic RECKLI®-Formliners. Their elasticity, quality and reusability contribute to the aesthetics and the economic efficiency of the whole process and make it possible to recreate the image onto the concrete surface.

RECKLI GmbH
Eschstrasse 30
D-44629 Herne
Germany

www.reckli.de
Tel: +39 (0)232-317-060
Fax: +39 (0)232-317-0650
E-mail: info@reckli.de

The printed concrete pavement Impreton is an in situ set slab whose surface is colored with non-metallic hardeners, so that the material acquires the surface hardness and strength of stone. It is stamped with a mold in order to obtain the selected pattern and texture. Pavements may also be imprinted with non-slip designs. Printed pavements Impreton combine the strength, durability and flexibility of designs in concrete with the aesthetic characteristics of paving stones, bricks, slates and other materials.

One of the advantages of these pavements is their design flexibility. Given the product's application technique, different patterns, designs, colors and textures may be combined, with no limits to the possible options. Another advantage is its rapid application: both the pavement and the substrate are set in a single operation, at an approximate rate of 80 sqm per day.

Edfan
C/Juan de Austria 95-97 Ático 3 A
08018 - Barcelona
Spain

www.microcemento.com
Tel: +34 93-320-9092
Fax: +34 93-320-9093
E-mail: info@microcemento.com

Thincrete is a cementitious coating that can be aplied to floors and walls of both interiors and exteriors. It has a broad range of textures that immitate natural stones like slate, granite and others.

Thincrete can be aplied over existing surfaces without the need to remove any material. It is protected with sealants and easy to maintain.

Edfan
C/Juan de Austria 95-97 Ático 3 A
08018 - Barcelona
Spain

www.microcemento.com
Tel: +34 93-320-9092
Fax: +34 93-320-9093
E-mail: info@microcemento.com

Microcement

Edfan

Micro polished pavement

Microcement is a layer between 1 and 2 mm thick, applicable to floors, walls and furniture. Previous uses include environments such as: commercial stores, rural settings and city houses, apartments, and private garages and has attained optimum results. It has been used for exteriors as well as interiors with equally impressive results.

Placement versatility and the wide range of possible colors make Microcement an ideal material for interior architecture.

The advantages of Microcement are:

- Quick Placement: up to 50 sqm per day with just two people working on it.
- Quick transit release: in just a few hours.
- Colors: There are 34 available colors and special colors are also available on request.
- No need to remove floor: In most cases the Microcement can be placed over existent floors and walls.
- It does not require joints: which allows for continuous coating without cuts.
- Minimum Thickness: between 1 and 2 mm thick, thus avoiding level differences with surroundings.

Edfan
C/Juan de Austria 95-97 Ático 3 A
08018 - Barcelona
Spain

www.microcemento.com
Tel: +34 93-320-9092
Fax: +34 93-320-9093
E-mail: info@microcemento.com

The ArmourColor range can create the perfect interior for all functional and design requirements, and make ideal wall coverings for private and public use, particularly in high traffic areas. Highly versatile and robust, the finishes are scrub resistant, breathable and comply with both UK and American fire classification requirements. Producing impressive interiors which combine color and durability, they add personality to any space.

The range, which includes BaseColors and protective Clearseal coatings, can be applied to a wide range of substrates including concrete, plaster and brick.

Perlata: Perlata is an elegant finish with a subtle sparkle or shimmer, creating visual texture and directional effect. The finish is dependent on the hand of the applicator, creating a unique and visually striking wall coating at close quarters, yet subtle when viewed from a distance.

Tactite: a high performance solution for demanding interiors, Tactite creates a tough, durable and hygienic wall coating. The finish is exceptionally hardwearing, easy to clean and includes anti-bacterial properties to prevent mould and bacterial growth. Tactite is highly suitable for commercial interiors such as hospitals, schools, offices and high traffic public areas where cleanliness is essential. Also ideal for domestic use, Tactite features a 'soft touch' feel to create a warm, inviting interior with a suede or textured finish.

Armourcoat Surface Finishes
Morewood Close, London Road,
Sevenoaks
Kent TN13 2HU
United Kingdom

www.armourcoat.com
Tel: +44 (0) 173-246-0668
Fax: +44 (0) 173-245-0930
E-mail: sales@armourcoat.co.uk

Sculptural™ walls are constructed from a series of pre-cast panels that are bonded to the substrate. The panel joints are then filled and sanded and a final decoration is applied to the surface. Sculptural™ designs are created by combining computer-aided design with traditional hand sculpting to create designs that fit together with total accuracy yet retain the essence of being hand crafted. Some of the designs are based on a single panel that creates a repeating pattern; others are made from a sequence of different panels that can be integrated together in many different ways to create totally unique sculpted walls. The multiple panel designs make it possible to create non-repetitive seamless sculptural walls where the designs flow and change across the surface just as in nature. As a consequence, no two walls need ever be identical. Sculptural™ panels are mineral based and incorporate up to 30% post-consumer recycled content (depending on design), are non-toxic and are completely non-combustible. The panels are extremely dense and hard with a smooth ceramic-like surface. Once the panels are installed each design can be finished in a range of decorative surface finishes. Some of the designs have been modeled in such a way as to enable the application of Armourcoat polished plaster finishes whilst other designs are more suited to a sprayed finish.

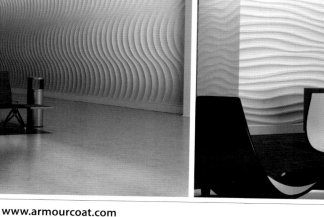

Armourcoat Surface Finishes
Morewood Close, London Road,
Sevenoaks
Kent TN13 2HU
United Kingdom

www.armourcoat.com
Tel: +44 (0) 173-246-0668
Fax: +44 (0) 173-245-0930
E-mail: sales@armourcoat.co.uk

StoLotusan Color

Sto

Façade paint featuring the Lotus effect

The Lotus effect is a natural phenomenon discovered on the Asian lotus plant. After each rainfall this plant's leaves are immaculately clean and dry, as they are not wettable with water; dirt runs off with the raindrops. This self-cleaning capacity is based on a micro-structure which minimizes the contact area between the leaf on the one hand and dirt and water on the other. As the leaf surface is also highly water-repellent, droplets of water roll off the surface immediately, taking loose dirt particles with them.

The StoLotusan Color façade paint is the first technical product to incorporate this phenomenon, which was christened the Lotus Effect® by its discoverer, the botanist Dr. Wilhelm Barthlott. Façades treated with this product remain dry and attractive for longer. The new surface technology also reduces the risk of attack by micro-organisms. Algae and fungal spores are either washed off or are unable to survive on a dry and dirt-free façade.

Lotusan is a façade paint with a matt, mineral look which can be finished in many colors of the StoColor System. StoLotusan Color enables simple, seamless application and offers good permeability for water vapor and carbon dioxide. The StoLotusan Color G variant is additionally provided with film conservation to combat algae and fungi. Designed especially for difficult locations (shaded, on the edge of woodland ...), this variant is even more effective in delaying colonisation by microorganisms. The combination of film conservation and natural protection employing the properties of the lotus leaf thus offers maximum protection from "uninvited guests" on façades.

1. Façade surface coated with Lotusan.
2. How the Lotus Effect works: Sto Lotusan Color's microtextured surface reduces the contact area for dirt particles and water. Thanks to the additional water-repellent properties, raindrops immediately roll off, taking loosely attached particles with them.

Sto AG
Ehrenbachstraße 1
D-79780 Stühlingen
Germany

www.sto.de
Tel: +39 (0) 774-457-1020
Fax: +39 (0) 774-457-2020
E-mail: infoservice@stoeu.com

COL.9®, a novel nanobinder from BASF for facade coatings, emulates the example of biominerals like bone and dental enamel. COL.9® is a dispersion of organic plastic polymer particles in which nanoscale particles of silica, the basic constituent of glass and quartz, are incorporated and evenly distributed. Thanks to this combination of elastic organic material and hard mineral, COL.9® based coatings combine the different advantages of conventional coating types. For example, unlike brittle, mineral based coatings, the widely used synthetic resin based dispersion paints are highly crack-resistant. But in summer, when dark house walls reach temperatures of 80° C and above in the sun, these coatings betray their weakness: on exposure to heat the synthetic resin begins to soften, and particles of soot and other contaminants stick to their surface. Because of its high silica content, however, the nanocomposite of COL.9® doesn't have this thermoplastic tackiness. At the same time, the mineral particles provide the coating with a hydrophilic i.e. water attracting surface on which raindrops are immediately dispersed. As regards cleanliness, this offers a dual benefit: in heavy rain, particles of dirt are washed off extensively from the façade surface. Also, the thin film of water remaining when the rain has stopped dries extremely quickly, which prevents mold formation. In contrast, the rain rolling off unevenly in thick droplets from water-repellent surfaces of fully synthetic resin coatings often leaves behind unattractive streaks of dirt.

1. Inorganic nanoparticles homogeneously incorporated and fixed in organic polymer particles provide ideal features for facade coatings. Image: BASF - The Chemical Company, 2008
2. Single family house in Viersen (Germany): The approx. 700 m² facade of this house was painted completely with Herbol-Symbiotec® in October 2007. Photo: Akzo Nobel

www.basf.com
Tel: +49 (0)621-600
Fax: +49 (0)621-604-2525

Ceramics

Ceramics are among the world's most ancient construction materials. They have been used continuously for thousands of years in many different ways. Even today they are still used, mostly in their traditional forms of bricks and tiles. The disconnection between exterior surface and interior structure produced by modern construction systems has created a great interest for decorative surface finishes. Ceramic tiles and bricks are very important in this context and many beautiful designs are available. Today ceramic materials are being developed for the most high-tech applications. Piezo-electric ceramics that create electrical current when they receive mechanical pressure are used in technical applications. Shape-memory and bio-ceramics play an ever increasing role in medicine. Although not many of these technologies have reached the field of architecture and construction, today there are many ceramic tiles available with self-cleaning, pollution reducing and anti-bacterial properties.

Classification of ceramic products

Clay Type	Type of Ceramic	Piece	Composition	Porosity and absorption
Ordinary (illites)	Floor tile	Bricks Barrel tiles Floor tiles	By hand	Very high
Selected and measured (illites)	Industrial	Bricks Roof tiles of all types Floor tiles With little shaping	Rows	High
Selected, measured, smooth with fine grain	Industrial	Intricately shaped Air and smoke ducts	Rows	High
		Floor tiles	Laminated	
Selected, measured, smooth with very fine grain	Faience	Figures, molding Decorative overlays	Molded	Medium
		Glazed tiles	Pressed	Impermeable
		Low quality bathroom pieces	Molded	
Refractory	Refractory	Pieces for cladding ovens, fireplaces, etc	Pressed	Medium
Non-refractory, pliable, very fine	Stoneware	Quality bathroom pieces	Molded	Very low
		Floor tiles Finishes	Pressed	
Kaolin	Vitreous porcelain	Quality bathroom pieces	Molded	Impermeable

I Frammenti

Brix - Claudio Silvestrin

Small mosaic tiles

The "I Frammenti" line of mosaic tiles consists of 30x30 cm modules, each one containing 2304 5 mm micro-cubes, mounted randomly on backing mesh. The small size of the cubes creates a continuous surface with no joins visible and able to take any form.

The tiles are available in two vaiants, one (Mix) that is naturally matt ina appearance and another (Gloss) where the tiles have a gloss coating that makes them bright and shiny. Each variation can be either monochromatic or have a blend of three colors that create a lively surface.

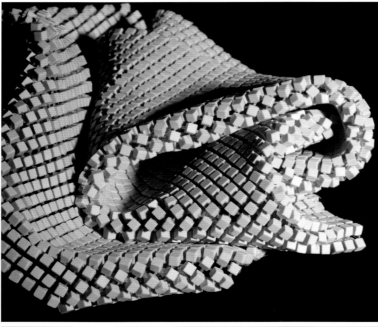

BRIX s.r.l.
Via Circonvallazione N/E, 116
41049, Sassuolo, Modena
Italy

www.brixweb.com
Tel: +39 053-681-2426
Fax: +39 053-681-2680
E-mail: info@brixweb.com

The Caudex series (Lat. "trunk") was developed thanks to a rediscovered desire for intimacy and naturalness. Wood conveys this feeling, and Caudex echoes it - not as an imitation but rather a contemporary ceramic interpretation. Its distinguishing feature is the interplay of very slightly varying nuances of the respective color (wenge, graphite or cognac). The desired effect is emphasized by the formats of 11 × 90, 15 × 90 and 22.5 × 90 cm. These board- or panel-like dimensions offer numerous options. Whether laid as irregular mixed bond with all the three sizes or regular laying with only one format: the result is always a finish full of warmth, which creates a pleasant environment. It is also extremely versatile with regard to different styles: Caudex suits a modern loft, ethno-mix elements or even more rural settings.

Deutsche Steinzeug Keramik GmbH
Postfach 49
92515 Schwarzenfeld
Germany

www.agrob-buchtal.de
E-mail: agrob-buchtal@deutsche-steinzeug.de

Concrete series

Agrob Buchtal

Ceramic tiles with embedded crystals

This creation presents itself as an integral complete solution for walls and floors. The series follows the trend towards horizontal laying with the large format of 30 × 60 cm. The surface is reminiscent of a modern concrete interpretation or fine plastering techniques and harmonizes in noble silver-grey with a reduced room design. Sand-beige, on the other hand, underlines a warm, elegant ambience. As regards the decors, Stone and Stars offer emotional design variants. Stone combines various natural stones in beige and brown with a turquoise-colored artificial stone to form a jointless color row. Stars fascinates with Swarovski crystals in different places and sizes. In the graphite-colored decorative element, they sparkle like stars, and the colors, refined with lustre, underscore the feeling of luxury. The decors Screen and Stripes, which emphasize a geometric and puristic architectural design, stand for the opposite style. While Screen includes the join due to its grid of rectangles, Stripes obtains this effect by asymmetric lines.

Deutsche Steinzeug Keramik GmbH
Postfach 49
92515 Schwarzenfeld
Germany

www.agrob-buchtal.de
E-mail: agrob-buchtal@deutsche-steinzeug.de

This series offers numerous design possibilities for representative areas such as hotels, foyers, banks, administration buildings or in the catering trade. A very wide color range makes this possible: it comprises both neutral and warm shades and extends from light to dark. Geo has a structure resembling travertine, and the tile body in matching color is an integral part of the surface look. Thanks to this interaction, a special mixture of archaic naturalness and rough charm is created - an ideal basis for perfect "public presentations". Immense creative scope is offered by sophisticated architectural design elements: in the case of Quadro, regularly arranged small metal squares are integrated in the tile. Thus, this solution is suitable e.g. for strictly geometric concepts which can be further varied by matching aluminum sticks or special steel strips. The border Logimas, on the other hand, pick up typographic elements in the form of figures represented concretely or abstractly. This results in artistic effects which combine playful ease with striking presence.

Deutsche Steinzeug Keramik GmbH
Postfach 49
92515 Schwarzenfeld
Germany

www.agrob-buchtal.de
E-mail: agrob-buchtal@deutsche-steinzeug.de

Chroma II series

Agrob Buchtal

Ceramic tiles series

The series Chroma II meets current trends in architecture: 46 colors that can be combined permit both finely shaded solutions and interesting contrasts. In addition, the silky-matt surfaces are suitable for rooms in which medical lasers are used. The sizes and the numerous special pieces are also matched to one another and thus are ideal for combination. Architectural accents are set by the large sizes of 25 × 50, 37.5 × 75 and 50 × 100, the strip tile sizes of 5.6 × 50, 12.5 × 100 cm and the high and deep relief tiles, which permit subtle light-shadow-effects. The system is rounded off by matching glass borders. Moreover, Chroma II harmonizes with the other series of the System Chroma. In this way, planners and architects can choose from among 87 different color variations.

Matching the color spheres vigorous, fresh, pure and warm, the mosaic mix is ideal above all for the design of walls – also in swimming pools and wellness zones – as well as for curves and columns. All colors perfectly harmonize with the other series of the System Chroma. Thanks to the film glued on the face side, it is equally suitable for use under water and in very wet areas. Perfect hygiene without effort is guaranteed by the Hydrotect surface coating.

Deutsche Steinzeug Keramik GmbH

Postfach 49

92515 Schwarzenfeld

Germany

www.agrob-buchtal.de

E-mail: agrob-buchtal@deutsche-steinzeug.de

Lace Tile

The Third Nature - Jethro Macey

Tile with 3-dimensional lace pattern

By mixing conventional materials with high technology surface design techniques a repeating pattern is translated from lace into a three dimensional tile.

The tiles reveal the decorative rose pattern when laid in multiples. Cast in concrete the tiles are suitable for interior and exterior applications.

Projects include Urban outfitters, Revolution Vodka Bar and private residences in the UK and Europe.

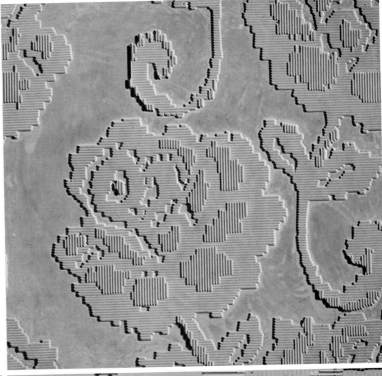

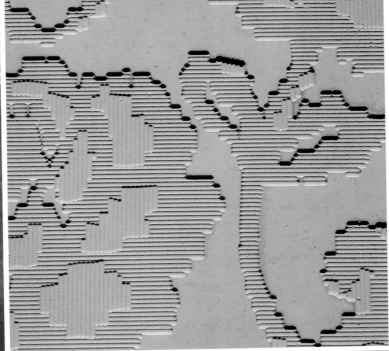

The Third Nature
Suhaili
Truro, TR4 8RW
UK

www.thethirdnature.co.uk
Tel: +44 (0) 790-969-5204
E-mail: info@thethirdnature.co.uk

Jethro Macey
3a Waterside House
Falmouth Road
Penryn, Cornwall, TR108BG
UK

www.jethromacey.com
Tel: +44 (0) 781-393-0219
E-mail: jethro@jethromacey.com

Architects often ask themselves, how can this surface, this wall or floor, give more? What more can it give? This series of ceramic wall tiles answers the question. The tiles reach out to touch and be touched.

Much like appropriating found objects, these tiles are made using the found spaces between bodies and architectural surfaces, and turned into positive forms. The design process is incidental; the forms happen, they aren't sculpted or orchestrated. The resulting tiles are a formal hybrid between two very necessary and basic architectural elements, the body and the wall. Part body and part wall, the tiles echo the presence of a person, a posture, and literally reach-out to be touched.

What these tiles give is a reference to the human body, embedded in a building material. The tiles encourage direct physical interaction with walls. Through touching and leaning, bodies find new niches for support, undulating folds and protrusions for resting, stimulating pressure points, or simply fitting like a garment - a new-found intimacy.

Made in posture and/or body-specific clusters, the tiles are designed in standard finished dimensions, to be incorporated into 15 × 15cm tiled surfaces. With the ability to be integrated into otherwise standard and inexpensive tiled surfaces, Found Space Tiles function, on one level, exactly like any other ceramic wall tile. What sets them apart is their added value, their generosity in offering wall surface area that supports the body in leaning and resting positions.

touchy-feely - Stephanie Davidson - Georg Rafailidis

Ossastr.15
D-12045 Berlin
Germany

www.touchy-feely.net
Tel: +49 (0)302-634-3990
Fax: +49 (0)302-634-3992
E-mail: info@touchy-feely.net

Bioessenze - Haute Couture

Lea Ceramiche

Textured ceramic tiles

The characteristic grain of the wood differs every time in the Bioessenze collection and makes any wall or floor surface suggestive, varied and balanced. Bioessenze allows the use of wood tiles anywhere as it is resistant to wear and tear, atmospheric agents and does not require maintenance even after several years. It is not affected by scratches or damp, is easy to fit and long-lasting. Bioessenze is obtained by means of a safe production cycle that fully respects the environment since it does not emit pollutants into the atmosphere and water. It uses widely available natural resources, no trees are felled and it recycles ceramic waste from manufacturing at an amount of 20% of its weight. Bioessenze is produced using the revolutionary LEA FULL HD technology, that combines Lea Ceramiche's know-how and digital decoration. Each item produced expresses an impressive, pure naturalness due to the number of pieces, each different from the others, which could never have been reproduced with previous technologies.

Haute Couture is a collection of tiles realized in honed grès porcelain that dresses any type of environment with discretion and elegance, thanks to its skin texture and neutral colors that are well suited to many furniture styles. It is perfectly in line with contemporary furniture and design trends.

Lea Ceramiche
Via Cameazzo, 21
41042 Fiorano modenese (Mo)
Italy

www.ceramichelea.it
Tel: +39 053-683-7811
Fax: +39 053-683-0326, +39 053-683-2827
E-mail: info@ceramichelea.it

Mosa has revived a design classic from the Sixties: the Kho Liang Ie Collection. Gloss white tiles with a relief of circles, segments of circles, diagonals and triangles. Size 10 × 10 cm.

The relief tiles can be combined to create unusual effects. A smooth wall tile is also available to complement the relief tiles.

Kho Liang Ie (1927-1975) was one of the most significant interior and industrial designers in the Netherlands. During his all too short career, Kho managed to create an impressive oeuvre. He was a designer of immeasurable value to furniture manufacturers like Artifort, CAR and Spectrum. In the Sixties he used the relief tiles he had designed for Mosa in the interior of Schiphol International Airport.

Royal Mosa
Meerssenerweg 358
6224 AL Maastricht
The Netherlands

www.mosa.nl
Tel: +31 (0) 43-368-9444
Fax: +31 (0) 43-368-9333
E-mail: servicedesk@mosa.nl

Paliogen, Lumogen, Sicopal

BASF

Black paint that does not absorbe heat

Dark surfaces of building roofs and façades attract the heat, but light surfaces remain distinctly cooler because dark surfaces absorb the incident sunlight and convert it into heat, while light surfaces reflect most of the incoming energy.

Although these physical principles at first appear unalterable, innovative pigments from BASF nevertheless make it possible for surfaces to heat up much less in the sun despite their dark color: Paliogen® Black, Lumogen® Black and Sicopal® Black. In contrast to carbon black, the standard black pigments, they reflect most of the invisible near infrared (NIR) radiation which accounts for more than 50 percent of the total incident solar energy.

But these paints offer heat-reducing benefits not only as pigments in purely black surfaces: paints, coatings and plastics in almost all other color shades also contain greater or lesser amounts of black pigments. If the BASF black pigments are used instead of carbon black, these colors also heat up much less in the sun.

The demand for NIR-reflecting black pigments for paints and coatings is constantly growing. There are many applications for these "cool paints", ranging from roofs through façades to metal containers for international shipping traffic to protect their contents against the searing tropical sun. And their use is not restricted to coatings, because the pigments are also suitable for coloring plastics. As representatives of the organic pigments, the Lumogen® Black range of pigments are recommended for use in plastics because of their greater temperature stability. This opens up many possibilities for plastic paneling, window frames, not forgetting the entire interior trim of vehicles.

1-2. BASF House, a low-energy construction project in Nottingham, UK, demonstrates the benefits of modern construction chemicals. The coating of the roof contains heat-reflecting pigments which significantly lower the temperatures. Images: BASF - The Chemical Company, 2008

www.basf.com
Tel: +49 (0)621-600
Fax: +49 (0)621-604-2525

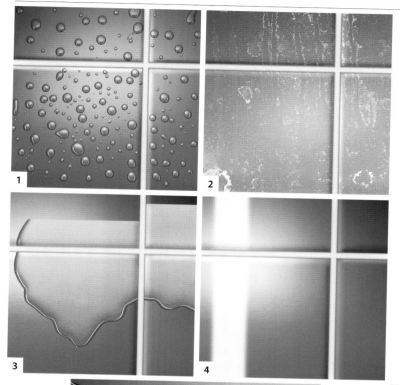

1

2

3

4

This innovation is unique in its form, which is not based on a lotus effect, but on a special principle of action: titanium dioxide is baked onto the glaze of the tiles as a catalyst, which generates a reaction between light, oxygen and air humidity. This photocatalytic effect is activated by normal indoor lighting. The coating is not simply applied by spraying or any other "cold" method, but baked onto the glaze at high temperatures. Hydrotect is so robust that it can be used not only for wall but also for floor tiles. This surface coating lends ceramic tiles amazing properties:

• Extremely easy to clean: water is not repelled, but spreads to form a thin film on the surface. In this way, dirt is washed down and can be easily removed.

• Antibacterial effect: The photocatalysis produces activated oxygen, which decomposes microorganisms such as bacteria, fungi, algae, moss and germs and prevents the formation of new pathogenes. While the effect decreases in the case of other methods based on the addition of certain additives, the antibacterial effect of Hydrotect reactivates itself again and again.

• Eliminates unwelcome or harmful odors. This applies both indoors and outdoors, e.g. to the exhaust fumes produced by industry and cars: Scientific analyses prove that a Hydrotect façade surface of 1000 sqm cleans the air as effectively as 70 medium-sized deciduous trees.

1-2. With conventional tiles water drops form and dirt is left on the surface after drying.

3-4. With Hydrotect water spreads as a thin film on the surface and washes dirt down which can be easily removed.

5. Rainwater follows this principle so that Hydrotect's self-washing-effect effectively supports the perfect look of the building shell.

6. Hydrotect can be also used for humid interior spaces making them easy to clean, while having an antibacterial effect and eliminating disagreeable odors.

5

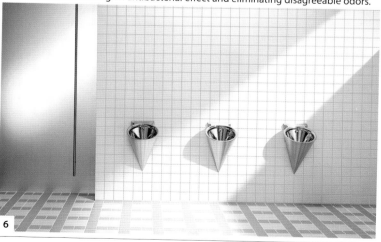

6

Deutsche Steinzeug Keramik GmbH
Postfach 49
92515 Schwarzenfeld
Germany

www.agrob-buchtal.de
E-mail: fassade@deutsche-steinzeug.de

KerAion façades comply with official standards and – thanks to their practically unlimited durability – are very economical. The open joints ensure an optimal rear ventilation, and its low weight makes KerAion particularly suitable for anchoring in critical outside wall layers. KerAion can be used with different mounting systems such as K8, Quadro and SikaTack®.

KerAion and the visible clamp system K8 form a unit in the mounting of façade ceramics, which has been used for decades. The clamp system K8 owes its great popularity to the wide field of applications for all commercially available substructures and its simple, quick mounting. The system K8 consists of different stainless steel clamps, whose functions are precisely matched. The KerAion façade panels are safely fixed onto the substructure by means of the stainless steel clamps. To prevent clattering and constraining forces in the case of alternating wind loads, the façade panels are installed on the substructure in a non rigid way. The different clamp variations can be supplied in bright stainless steel or completely or partially powder-coated.

The economical SikaTack®-Panel system is a glueing system for the hidden and stress-free mounting of façade panels. It consists of the permanently elastic SikaTack®-Panel glue, the SikaTack®-Panel mounting tape, which is self-adhesive on both sides, for fixing the panels, as well as the corresponding products for the pre-treatment of the bases.

With the SikaTack®-Panel system façade panels are invisibly fastened on commercially available substructures.

1

2

1-4. Façades covered with KerAion ceramic panels.

5. KerAion with clamp fastening K8.

6. KerAion wall construction SikaTack ®

Deutsche Steinzeug Keramik GmbH

Postfach 49
92515 Schwarzenfeld
Germany

www.agrob-buchtal.de
E-mail: agrob-buchtal@deutsche-steinzeug.de

Zero

Vandersanden

Brick masonry without jointing

With Zero®, brick producer Vandersanden has developed a new facing brick to easily create a modern façade. The innovation allows a joint-free look with traditional masonry. The secret lies in a recess at the top of the facing brick.

In modern architecture, the goal is often to create homogenous façade surfaces by limiting the jointing. Until now, this was only possible by gluing or thin-layer mortar. However, the disadvantage of these techniques is the high threshold to use them, given that it is not traditional masonry.

Zero® changes this for once and for all. The new facing brick allows the use of traditional masonry to achieve a homogenous brick façade with almost no jointing. Thanks to a recess at the top of the facing brick, the mortar largely sinks into the brick. This results in a jointing look of just 4 mm.

Technical advisor Ivan d'Hanis clarifies: "What's great about Zero® is that the facing brick is processed according to the traditional masonry method. The contractor also uses a profile, rope, trowel and mortar. The only difference with laying a traditional brick is the placement of the mortar and the tilting method. The mortar is placed in the recess of the facing brick. Then, the next brick is pressed down at the front on top of the row below and tilted backwards, which presses down the mortar. Possible residue can be scraped away at the back. As a result, the front of the brick always remains clean."

In addition to the clean aesthetic look, Zero® also offers some other advantages. Zero® is also cost saving, given that jointing is no longer needed. The result can be seen instantly. Due to the lack of jointing, the façade will age more slowly.

Vandersanden Plc
Nijverheidslaan 11
3650 Lanklaar
Belgium

www.vandersanden.com
www.zerobrick.be
Tel.: +32 89 79 02 50
Fax.: +32 89 75 41 90
E-mail: info@vandersanden.be

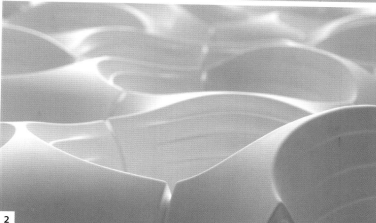

elegant embellishments, presents a new prototype of proSolve370e: decorative, depolluting architectural tiles.

The proSolve370e prototype is composed of approximately 55 photocatalytic tiles, to form a 10 sqm suspended screen. The tiles are produced at 40% of their intended size, indicating their primary use: as a building façade element.

proSolve370e is a decorative architectural tile that can effectively reduce air pollution from traffic in cities when installed near traffic ways or on building façades. The tiles are coated with a superfine titanium dioxide (TiO_2), a pollution-fighting technology that is activated by ambient daylight. This is the nano photocatalytic version of conventional TiO_2 commonly used as pigment and known for its self-cleaning and germicidal qualities. It requires only small amounts of naturally occurring UV light and humidity to effectively reduce air pollutants into harmless amounts of carbon dioxide and water. When positioned near pollution sources, the coated tiles break down and neutralize NOx (nitrogen oxides) and VOCs (volatile organic compounds) directly where they are generated. As a modification to existing architectural surfaces, proSolve370e essentially "tunes buildings" to respond better to their immediate environments.

The design of the tiles is generated to maximize the coating technology, achieving new levels of surface area and complexity, capturing omni-directional light where light is dense or scarce. The sculptural surfaces maintain an inherent synergy between design form and the molecular technology, each informing the other in the process. As a result, the tiles incorporate an elegant technology, while remaining, formally, a decorative apparatus.

1. Prototypes of the Prosolve 420 series were exhibited at the 11th International Architecture Exhibition, Venice Biennale 2008, as part of "Updating Germany: Projects for a Better Future", an exhibition at the German Pavilion.
2. Detail of the Prosolve 420 prototypes.
3. De-polluting installation around a city-owned tree, London Architecture Biennale 2006, based on a cylindrical derivation of the Penrose parquet.

**elegant embellishments
dring und schwaag gbr**
Axel-Springer-Straße 39
D-10969 Berlin
Germany

www.elegantembellishments.net
Tel: +49 (0) 303-034-5003
E-mail: info@elegantembellishments.net

Hyperwave

Limestone Gallery

Natural stone panels with 3-d carved designs

Hyperwave by Testi is a range of flowing 3D designs, carved into natural stone slabs, that can be customized to each project with a choice of materials and finishes. Any stone can be specified, subject to the material's suitability to the innovative new process, with the option of a honed, milled or polished finish.

Suitable for interior and exterior application, the range is offered in standard size panels of 400 × 400 × 30 mm and 700 × 700 × 30 mm or single slabs up to a maximum of 2800 × 1600 × 30 mm. The pattern can be repeated without limit for any height or length or can be incorporated into an individual shower panel and tray.

LimeStone Gallery Ltd
Arch 47 South Lambeth Road
London SW8 1SS
UK

www.limestonegallery.co.uk
Tel: +44 (0) 207-735-8555
Fax: +44 (0) 207-793-8880
E-mail: info@limestonegallery.com

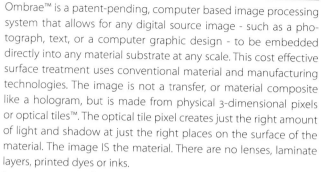

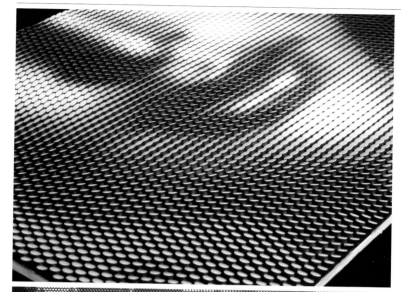

Ombrae™ is a patent-pending, computer based image processing system that allows for any digital source image - such as a photograph, text, or a computer graphic design - to be embedded directly into any material substrate at any scale. This cost effective surface treatment uses conventional material and manufacturing technologies. The image is not a transfer, or material composite like a hologram, but is made from physical 3-dimensional pixels or optical tiles™. The optical tile pixel creates just the right amount of light and shadow at just the right places on the surface of the material. The image IS the material. There are no lenses, laminate layers, printed dyes or inks.

Images are created by casting and/or machining into glass, resin, plastics, stone and cast stone, concrete, metal, leather, vinyl, rubber, composites, fabrics and more for uses in architectural settings, industrial and product design, and a myriad of commercial applications. The Ombrae™ system allows designers to consider an unlimited range of opportunity. A designer's imagination is the only limitation of the Ombrae™ system.

A key feature of the Ombrae system is the ability to "brand" surfaces across different materials so that the design space has a theme and a style all its own – unique to the customer and the environment. Ombrae technology is very effective in settings where designers want to "send a message" or "transmit a theme" in the very surfaces of the space itself. These themes or messages can be carried throughout the space, interior to exterior, walls to ceilings to floors to counter tops, packaging and display, down to the very carpet and the furniture. This ability to carry a design across multiple materials is a highly sought but often unattainable design feature that Ombrae is able to provide. Our exclusive services examine a given application in terms of lighting conditions and viewing perspectives to ensure each installation is a perfect fit.

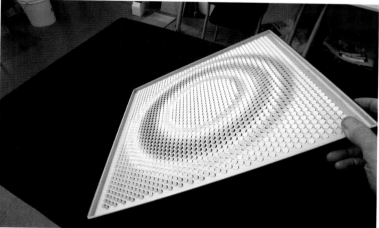

Ombrae Studios Inc.
Studio 3-1334 Odlum Drive
Vancouver, British Columbia, V5L 3M3
Canada

www.ombrae.com
Tel: +1 604-255-9929
E-mail: info@ombrae.com

Metals have been used for millennia and continue today to be important in modern material technologies. In architecture, metals started to play a prominent role only after their industrialized production became possible. Although metals have some excellent characteristics of strength, ductility, elasticity and isotropy they also have some ecological shortcomings that have been made apparent as architects have become more interested in such matters. The extraction and processing of metals are activities that require great amounts of energy and pollute the environment. At the same time developments in the fields of plastics, ceramics and wood processing have offered new alternatives to the use of metals. The most spectacular technical advances in metal technology have yet to find their way to architectural applications. Research is focused on the enhancement of strength, resilience and conductivity of electricity. In the field of construction the major goal is the creation of steels and other alloys with greater strength and lower weight that will allow the creation of lighter structures. Metal foams are starting to be used in architecture not only for their technical but also for their aesthetic properties. High quality (and high price) metals like stainless steel and titanium are also becoming more common in some small-scale applications. Titanium has also become important in the form of titanium dioxide as the basic material for the creation of pollution-reducing coatings and materials. Metal is also a common material in the development of digital fabrication techniques that allow the creation of very complex shapes.

Properties of metals used in construction

Name	Symbol	Density (kg/m³)	Young's modulus (kN/m³)	Shear modulus (kN/m³)	Bulk modulus (kN/m³)	Thermal conductivity (W/mK)
Aluminum	Al	2700	70	26	76	237
Chromium	Cr	7190	279	115	160	93.9
Copper	Cu	8940	110-128	48	140	401
Iron	Fe	7860	211	82	170	80.4
Lead	Pb	11300	16	5.6	46	35.3
Magnesium	Mg	1750	45	17	45	156
Nickel	Ni	8900	200	76	180	90.9
Tin	Sn	7310	50	18	58	66.8
Titanium	Ti	4500	116	44	110	21.9
Zinc	Zn	7140	108	43	70	116

SystemTecture is a System 180 brand name and represents the construction and joint technic utilized by System 180. Architect Jürg Steiner developed System 180 as a variable and flexible element for the realization of interior fittings and exhibition areas. The potential for this unique system to be expanded into modular furniture was quickly recognized. System 180 GmbH was created for the design and development, as well as production and distribution of this system.

System 180 now not only distributes modular furnishing systems, but also plans and realizes structural designs for architectural projects. Depending on the requirement, the joint elements can be produced in various measurements.

System 180's capacity spectrum reaches from staircases, bridges, façades and roof constructions to supporting frameworks and geodetic structures. The strength of SystemTecture lies in the individual and unique technical solutions for challenging tasks whether in complexity, functionality or creativity.

1. In the areaway of the Martin-Gropius-Bau, System 180 contrived a roof construction for the exhibition of abstract expressionist paintings.
2. Galleria nazionale d'arte moderna, Rome, Italy. For the period of the reconstruction of the National Gallery in Rome one of the inner courtyards was used for promotional events. The courtyard was covered with a roof structure constructed from System 180.
3. Helicoidal staircase build with the System 180.
4. Following the renovation of the chapel at the catholic university in Limburg, the area was assigned the use of a conference and quiet area for the lecturers. To achieve this System 180 created a 'room within a room' structure which divided the open space into various areas. A staircase was constructed in order to reach the former gallery.
5. Canopy for a swimming pool, La Coruña, Spain.
6. Geodesic dome constructed with System 180..

System 180 GmbH
Kärntener Straße 21
10827 Berlin
Germany

www.system180.com
Tel: +49 (0) 30-788-5841
Fax: +49 (0) 30-787-09160
E-mail: mail@systemtecture.com

XURF Systems

Haresh Lalvani and Milgo/Bufkin

Smooth rigid curved metal surfaces

XURF Systems, inspired by biological membranes, comprise products driven by the goal of fabricating continuously morphable smooth rigid curved surfaces.

XURF Systems, which embody a new patent pending invention that allows to expand any flat sheet material into a 3-dimensionally curved surface. This enables XURF Systems to shape-and-make architectural surfaces having varying compound curvature with relative ease.

Applications include interior and exterior architectural surfaces, structures, sculpture and a variety of design products. The patent pending XURF system was invented by Haresh Lalvani in 1998 and has been under development since with Milgo.

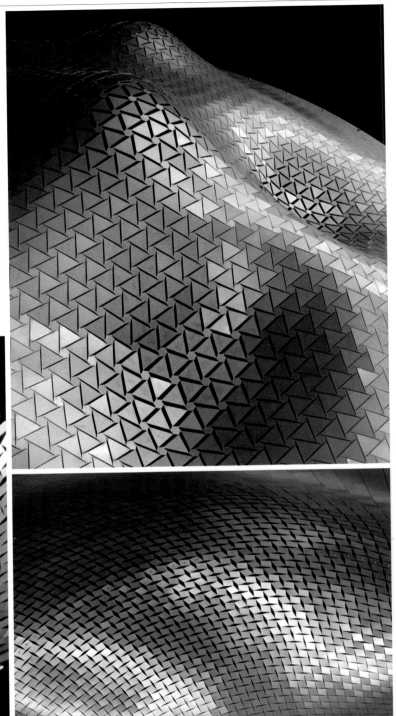

Milgo/Bufkin
68 Lombardy Street
Brooklyn, NY 11222
USA

www.milgo-bufkin.com
Tel: +1 718-388-6476
Fax: +1 718-963-0614
E-mail: info@milgobufkin.com

AlgoRhythms is the first family of products to grow out of the on-going collaboration between Haresh Lalvani and Milgo-Bufkin. AlgoRhythms comprise architectural surfaces and include available products like column covers, wall panels and ceiling systems as well as various utilitarian objects.

Dr. Haresh Lalvani, architect-morphologist and inventor of these new forms, states: *"AlgoRhythms proceed from the "bottom-up" and are based on morphologically structured information (meta architecture) that permits endless variations on a theme. The term "Algo-Rhythm" captures the flow, harmony and movement in the shape of the products as well as the use of generative procedures."*

AlgoRhythms are generated by an algorithmic approach combined with an economical method of digitally-driven fabrication, yielding mass-customized architectural surfaces. The 3-dimensionality of the curved surfaces, and their strength, "emerge" from flat sheets through a new "mass-customization" fabrication process in which each item can be produced differently and economically as when producing many identically. The wide range of unique forms produced this way are non-deformational, a special feature that maintains the integrity of metal sheet while curving it into three dimensions. The undulating look of these structures results from the behavior of a surface under force.

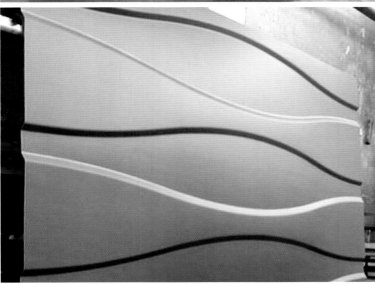

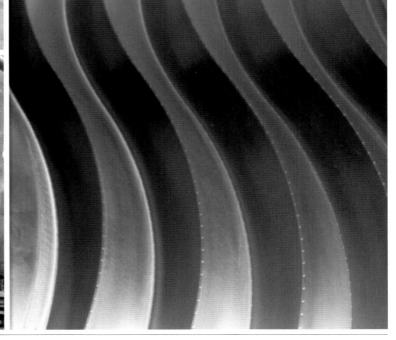

Milgo/Bufkin
68 Lombardy Street
Brooklyn, NY 11222
USA

www.milgo-bufkin.com
Tel: +1 718-388-6476
Fax: +1 718-963-0614
E-mail: info@milgobufkin.com

Alusion

Cymat

Stabilized aluminum foam panels

Visitors to the new Vancouver Convention Centre (VCC) expansion project in Vancouver, British Columbia, will be greeted in the main lobby by a wall made from a unique material: stabilized aluminum foam (SAF). Manufactured by Cymat Technologies Ltd. of Canada, and sold under the trade name Alusion™, the material offers designers and architects a variety of creative opportunities.

Alusion™ SAF is made by injecting air into molten aluminum, which contains a fine dispersion of ceramic particles. These particles stabilize the bubbles formed by the air, much like dry cocoa powder stabilizers bubbles when it is added to milk. The material can be made with up to 100% recycled aluminum and is manufactured in a number of versions.

Alusion™ is available in both a small-cell and a large-cell version, with either a natural finish or with open cells visible on one or both surfaces. Thicknesses range from 12.7 to 43.0 mm. The large-cell version with both sides open offers users a translucent material with an extraordinary texture. A 43-mm-thick version of large-cell Alusion™ was chosen for the wall at the VCC. Translucent versions of Alusion™ at trade shows and in other public spaces such as bars and restaurants, including a new restaurant facility in Spain. Due to its considerable strength, the small-cell version was selected by Audi as the surface used to display featured vehicles.

1

2

1. Meydenbauer Center, Bellevue Washington, USA.
2. Cafeteria Baluarte, Spain.
3. Vancouver Convention Centre, Canada
4. Detail shot of the Meydenbauer Center

3

4

Alusion
6320-2 Danville Rd.
Mississauga, Ontario, L5T 2L7
Canada

www.alusion.com
Tel: +1 905-696-2426
Fax: +1 905-696-9300
E-mail: info@alusion.com

W-ALL Fashion™ is an interior decorating system that is able to convey a precise image and that can easily be combined with other materials, designs and textures. The wall acquires aesthetic value through a sequence of modular panels that highlight the contemporary design of the installation. Every environment can be different from the next by mixing unique effects of colors and materials inserted with a sound geometry that enhances the rigor and simplicity of the project.

W-ALL Fashion™ is the outcome of combining a light and modular anodized aluminum structure with panels dressed with luxurious materials. The result is an interchangeable and easy-to-install system. The standard module is an 18"x18" square (45.7 x 45.7 cm) that can be customized in size, and allows for the creation of coverings for limited areas (one panel only) or for entire walls. When applied to large areas pre-fabricated structures are used instead of single modules.

The panels are made out of MDF or other supports such as aluminum over which the various finishes are applied. Because of their magnetic properties, the panels can be substituted and changed with extreme ease, according to personal creativity, without the need for structural intervention. All panels can be supplied with security supports that allow disassembly only by authorized personnel.

W-ALL
Borgo Giuseppe Mazzini 19
47011 Terra del Sole (FC)
Italy

www.w-all.it
Tel: +39 054-376-6405
Fax: +39 054-376-7034

Solucent
Cambridge Architectural

Metal meshes

Cambridge International is the world's largest manufacturer of woven metal products for industrial and architectural applications. Architectural mesh shading significantly improves building operations and occupant comfort. The highly sustainable and sophisticated nature of metal fabric makes it an ideal material for harnessing natural light. Cambridge Architectural metal fabric systems have long been known for transforming building façades and turning ordinary structures into signature landmarks. Cambridge Solucent shading systems save energy by shading the sun, optimize daylighting by selecting specific mesh patterns in specific building locations and achieve meaningful sustainable advantages as a material that is fully recyclable, virtually indestructible and maintenance-free. They can be fully integrated into curtain wall systems.

The varieties of opacities of Cambridge metal fabrics, combined with a wide selection of attachment hardware configurations, make Solucent mesh solar shading systems more versatile than any other daylighting method.

1

1. Arizona State University parking by Dick & Fritsche Design Group.
2. Carroll Creek Pedestrian Bridge by HNTB Architecture.
3. Attachment hardware: Curtain.
4. Tension attachment hardware: Eclipse.
5. Attachment hardware: Velocity. Installed at the Central Energy Plant for the Medical University of South Carolina by LS3P Associates.
6. Tension attachment hardware: Scroll.

2

Cambridge Architectural
105 Goodwill Rd
Cambridge, MD 21613
USA

www.cambridgearchitectural.com
Tel: +1 866-806-2385
E-mail: sales@cambridgearchitectural.com

eyetech

James & Taylor

Expanded metal cladding

James & Taylor have pioneered the use of this unique façade material, made by The Expanded Metal Company. The manufacturing process produces a 3-dimensional expanded aluminum mesh with a dual personality. Eyetech is opaque when viewed from one direction, transparent when viewed from the other, and it is this quality that is the key to its architectural appeal. It is an ideal material to give a modern, edgy feel to solid expanses of wall on large-scale buildings, and for environments that require high security at night and a robust exterior. Where eyetech really comes into its own in terms of functionality is on multi-storey car parks. It provides a secure, visually substantial surface while allowing the building to breathe without mechanical ventilation. It is increasingly being considered as a low-energy solar shading solution in hot countries. Despite its tough appearance, eyetech is almost chameleon-like in the way it constantly changes its appearance, depending on the surrounding light and color. It can also be layered to produce a moiré pattern effect, creating visual interest and wonderfully fluid surfaces on large stretches of wall. This is achieved with layers of slightly different sizes, one on top of the other. Lighting between the layers can give terrific night-time effects. The eyetech range of architectural systems combines this amazing material with clever and thoroughly engineered fixing solutions. Eyetech is available in an almost limitless range of sizes, material types and surface finishes. It's also environmentally friendly, as its unique expanding characteristics mean that the energy used to produce each square metre of cladding is kept to an absolute minimum.

1

1. Milton Keynes Hospital car park by Ingleton Wood LLP.
2. Detail of the Milton Keynes Hospital car park.
3. Young Vic theater in London by Haworth Tompkins.
4. The New Museum of Contemporary Art in New York by Kazuyo Sejima and Ryue Nishizawa/SANAA
5. View from the interior of the New Museum through the Eyetech mesh.

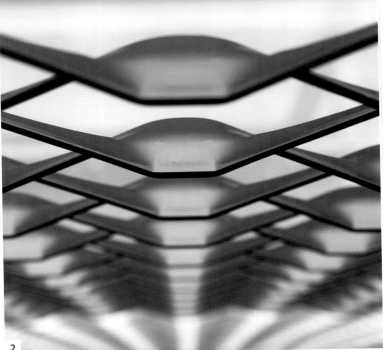

2

James & Taylor

Mitchell House
2 Montem Rd,
New Malden, Surrey KT3 3QW
UK

www.jamesandtaylor.co.uk
Tel: +44 (0) 208-942-3688
Fax: +44 (0) 208-336-2036
E-mail: info@jamesandtaylor.co.uk

3

4

5

Twentinox meshes

Twentinox

Metal fabrics

Twentinox manufactures metal fabrics for architectural applications for the exterior and interior. Most of Twentinox fabrics are made from stainless steel. Other materials such as bronze, silver, gold, aluminum are also available. The mesh is made from a round or flat wire, with colored, matt or glossy surface. All products are available from standard product lines. For particular optical effects and transparency the company produces at customers' specifications. Applications include wall and ceiling covers, room dividers, sunscreen, metal curtains, furniture, rolling doors.

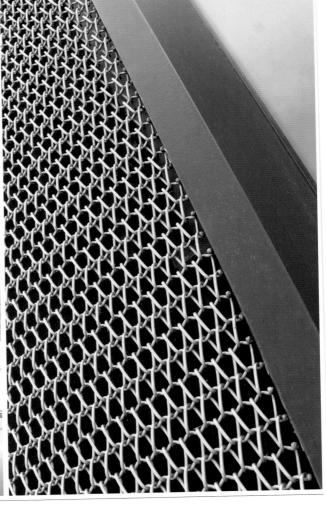

Twentinox
P.O. Box 6
7550 AA Hengelo Ov
The Netherlands

www.twentinox.com
Tel: +31 (0)74-291-6996
Fax: +31 (0)74-243-1659
E-mail: info@twentinox.com

Haver Architectural Wire Meshes couple aesthetic appearance with high technical qualities. They come in many different patterns, each with its own characteristics in terms of strength, transparency, metal density, surface finish and optical effect. High quality stainless steel with good corrosion resistance is the preferred material for buildings designed with architectural metal mesh.

Combining woven wire mesh with state-of-the-art LED technology, Imagic Weave enables the creation of individually programmable lighting effects in all colors including video presentations on a new or existing façade. By attaching LED-profiles to the reverse side of the wire mesh the homogenous and transparent look of the façade is maintained at all times, even when the LEDs are not in use.

1. Combining architectural mesh with latest LED technology for transparent media façades or other media applications. Photo: Haver & Boecker, Ralf Muckermann © Haver & Boecker.

2. Detail of Imagic Weave. Photo: Fototeam Walkenhorst © Haver & Boecker.

3. Aspire Tower, Doha. A landmark project being covered with 30.000 m² of architectural mesh. Photo: Pierre Sironval © Haver & Boecker.

4. Chesapeake Parking Garage. Stainless steel mesh offers a unique play with light and shadow as well as density and transparency. Photo: Hedrich Blessing Photographers © Haver & Boecker.

Haver & Boecker - Ralf Muckermann **www.weavingideas.com**

Ennigerloher Strasse 64
59302 Oelde
Germany

Tel: +49 25-223-00
Fax: +49 25-223-0404
E-mail: architektur@haverboecker.com

Beauty and strength are the features that distinguish this line. Steel Program is an antistatic, antiacid and antibacterical floor with a steel surface. It consists of a technical raised floor (a structure of inert wood or in calcium sulphate), covered with decorated or stiffened steel AISI 304 with a thickness of 0.8 mm. These tiles are also suitable for traditional laying, with adhesive.

For the surface, there is the possibility to choose among 28 decorations. These floors are very strong and suitable for very busy places. This line belongs to class 1 and is suitable in places whose temperatures range from -40° to +120°.

1. Steel Program plates on a raised floor.
2. Bathroom in the Puerta Aerica hotel in Madrid.
3-4. Staircases covered with Steel Program plates.

1

2

3

4

Bluestein S.R.L.
Viale Roma, 26
24011 Alme' (BG)
Italy

www.bluestein.it
Tel: +39 (0)35-637-952
Fax: +39 (0)35-547-1267
E-mail: info@bluestein.it

The Chicago architectural firm of Holabird & Root wished to appoint one of their headquarters conference rooms with a dashing twist: aluminum flooring.

After talking to a number of their contacts and other suppliers, they ended up at the door of Frank Pozdol. Pozdol's firm, Powerstrech, Inc, is a trusted supplier and installer of traditional floor coverings in the Chicago commercial flooring market. Pozdol was intrigued by the idea and surveyed a number of his industrial contacts for their opinions.

He commissioned some experiments and real-life test applications. Once he was satisfied with the results, he fabricated and installed Holabird & Root's aluminum floor. The positive response from the first architects and visitors encouraged Pozdol to continue his tests on the product.

Soon the Illinois Institute of Technology (IIT) announced the winner of its international competition to design two major new structures on its famous Ludwig Mies van der Rohe campus on Chicago's near South Side. Rem Koolhaas's Office of Metropolitan Architecture in Rotterdam was chosen for the new McCormick Tribune Campus Center.

Koolhaas created a partnership with Holabird & Root for design development and structural engineering. The conference room floor was actually an audition for the world's largest aluminum floor installation, over 30 000 expansive square feet in the common areas of the remarkable new Student Center.

The renowned project catapulted AlumaFloor and Frank Pozdol into the world's design and architectural spotlight.

Power Stretch, Inc. / Aluma Floor
740 Annoreno Drive
Addison, IL 60101
USA

www.aluminumfloors.com
Tel: +1 630-628-0226
Fax: +1 630-628-0230
E-mail: frankalumafloor@sbcglobal.net

Mosa Xtreme uniquely complements Mosa's architectural collection. The collection contains tiles in tempered glass, stainless steel and porcelain ceramic, all of which can be used individually and in combination with each other. These materials in a 30 × 30, 45 × 45 and 60 × 60 cm format open up possibilities for realizing ideas that will create a completely new look for commercial floors and walls. When selecting the new materials for these tiles, Mosa ensured that they were suitable for the usual methods of installation and that they could be cared for in the same way as regular ceramic tiles.

Xtreme Glass are tiles of tempered and normal non-tempered glass, provided with coating, for walls and indoor flooring in the residential and non-residential building sectors.

Xtreme Steel are stainless steel tiles, provided with ceramic carrier, for indoor flooring.

Xtreme Ceramics are porcelain quality ceramic tiles, for indoor and outdoor flooring.

Royal Mosa
Meerssenerweg 358
6224 AL Maastricht
The Netherlands

www.mosa.nl
Tel: +31 (0) 43-368-9444
Fax: +31 (0) 43-368-9333
E-mail: servicedesk@mosa.nl

Lineage tiles are made from solid stainless steel and bronze. They have a living finish, with no coatings or chemical patinas applied over the metal. The surface of Lineage tiles has been designed to mature with wear and to use the scratches and abrasions that occur with everyday use to its advantage.

While employing modern techniques to create Lineage tiles, the firm's design philosophy and processes are rooted in a strong sense of history. The inspiration for Lineage came largely from intaglio printmaking methods dating back to the 16th century.

Whether the tiles are used alone or as an accent to stone, tile, wood or glass, the enduring range of designs can transform any space into a truly memorable room that reflects personal styles and aesthetics. The tiles can be used in virtually any application: wet and dry, indoors and out, on walls and floors, countertops and fireplaces, showers, pools and even the highest traffic applications. The stainless steel range is rust-resistant and holds a beautiful luster. The customized bronze range was chosen for its attractive color, strength and natural patina. The combination of durability, beauty and flexibility make Lineage tiles a highly unique addition to any space.

Flux Studios, Inc.
4001 North Ravenswood Ave
Unit 603
Chicago, Illinois 60613
USA

www.fluxstudios.com
Tel: +1 773-883-2030
E-mail: fluxstudios@sbcglobal.net

cellscreen

korban/flaubert

Cellular structure - decorative/filter screen

Cellscreen is a cellular structure exploring rhythm, repetition and sequence that can be used as a free-standing screen. It is a simple, strong and elegant mathematical honeycomb in crisp lightweight aluminum.

There were various sources of inspiration for the creation of cell screen; tiling geometric patterns, natural patterns of packing and cracking as well as the decorative economy of patterns in Islamic architecture.

The aim of the designers was to produce a dense evocative structure from the simplest geometry, using a single line length and a repeated 5-way joint. This has generated a sequence of triangles and squares that optically form larger interlocking ovals and star shapes.

The final effect is transparent and simple from the front view but opaque, deep and complex from the angled approach.

A simple pattern generates an unfolding sequence of larger effects, suggesting motion and transformation while the interaction with light and shadow creates added complexity.

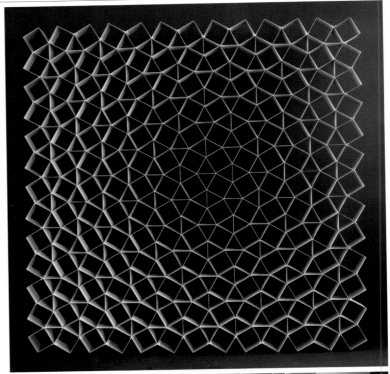

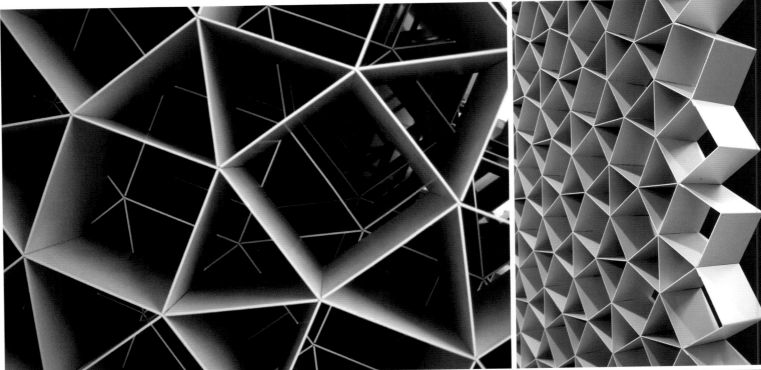

Korban/Flaubert Pty Ltd
8/8-10 Burrows Road
St Peters Nsw 2044
Australia

www.korbanflaubert.com.au
Tel/Fax: +61 29-557-6136
E-mail: info@korbanflaubert.com.au

Création Baumann offers a line of products which address the problems of energy efficiency and user comfort in glass buildings. To aid ergonomic styling of work stations, privacy screens with optimal glare and sun protection are in demand, as are heat efficient temperature controls to regulate the atmosphere of interiors.

The two prong approach sees the existing "Silver" collection optimized and enhanced. Setting it apart is a thin aluminum layer on the reverse of the fabric applied through a process which uses highly sophisticated engineering. Depending on its density, the textile retains a degree of sheerness. High sun reflection minimizes incoming light to create subdued, glare-free lighting whilst simultaneously minimizing the ingress of thermal energy. The "Silver" collection was enhanced with a protective coating making it more resistant to water stains, water vapours and dirt.

Fabrics from the "Steel" collection feature a thin layer of steel on the back. The application involves highly complex vacuum and nano technologies. Miniscule particles of steel are affixed by cathodic evaporation. Because steel is darker than aluminum, textiles from the steel collection reflect less sunlight than those from the "Silver" collection. In return they are washable and less susceptible to creasing and cracking. Another advantage of steel coated textiles is their great style diversity on woven and knitted fabrics. Thus designs encompass striped, lined and even burn-out motifs. All fabrics from the "Steel" collection are available in a width of three meters.

Outstanding results are achieved in functionality testing thanks to aluminum and steel coating that cannot be attained with conventional textiles. The entire group of the "Silver&Steel" collection has been submitted to comprehensive and rigorous evaluations.

Création Baumann
Bern-Zürich-Strasse 23
CH-4900 Langenthal
Switzerland

www.creationbaumann.com
Tel: +41 (0)62-919-6262
Fax: +41 (0)62-922-4547
E-mail: mail@creationbaumann.com

Although used for a long time, glass became a major architectural material in the 19th and 20th century. Today it is present as a façade material in huge quantities, providing buildings with ample natural light and views, but at the same time creating problems due to too much direct sunlight and its poor insulation qualities. Many new products focus on exactly these problems. Solar control glasses are available in many varieties from the technically simple introduction of louvers in a double glass panel to more sophisticated electrochromic glasses where transparency is controlled with the application of an electrical current. The insulating ability of glass can be augmented with the use of translucent double glass panels that incorporate either normal translucent insulating materials (glass fibers) or Aerogel. The surface effects that may be produced with glass have also been greatly amplified with the introduction of dichroic glasses, the perfection of colored glasses and the development of printing methods for glass. Translucent glasses are also available in many different forms, from white translucent glass to glasses incorporating textiles and other materials. At the higher end of the technological spectrum there are not only electrochromic and dichroic glasses but also anti-bacterial and self-cleaning ones.

Properties of float glass	
Density	2520 kg/m³
Resistance to tension	35-55 N/mm²
Resistance to compression	3800-4670 N/mm²
Coefficient of thermal expansion	23×10^{-6} K^{-1}
Thermal conductivity	0,7-1,1 W/m°C

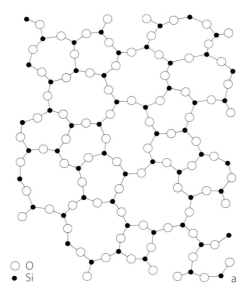
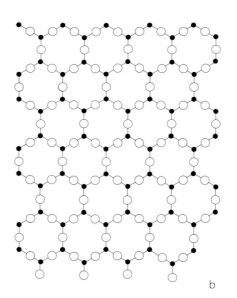

○ O
● Si

Structure of glass (a) and quartz (b) SiO2.

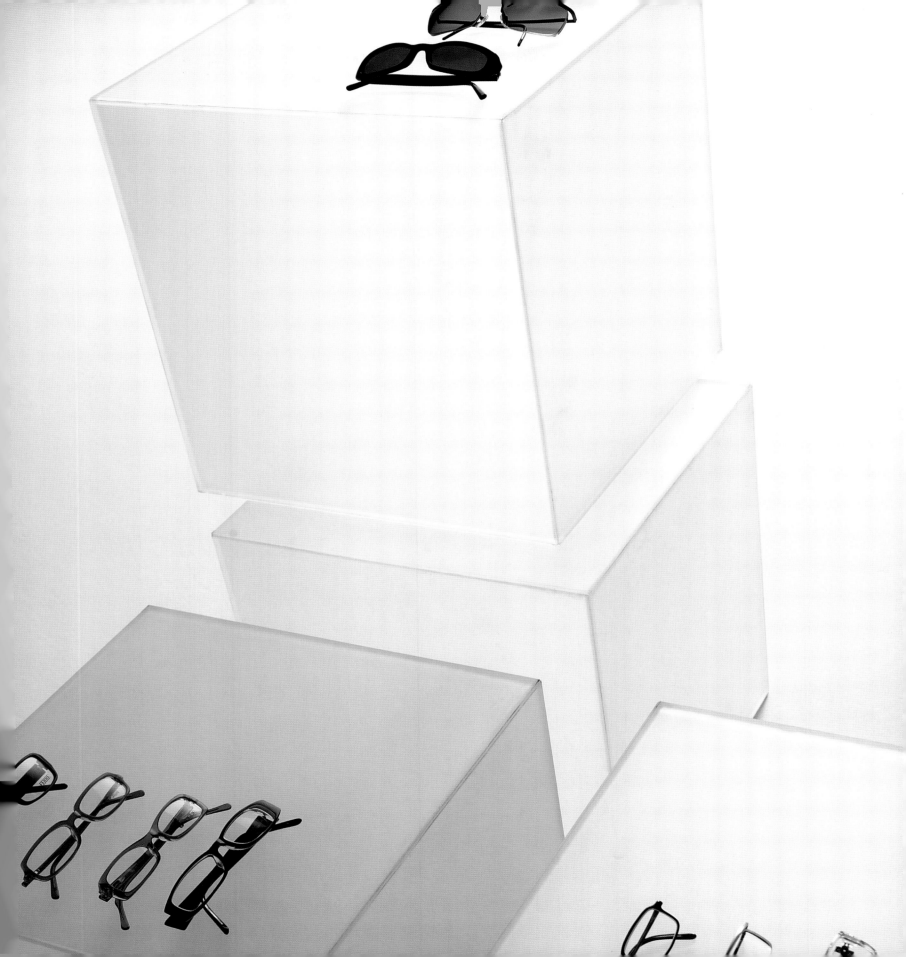

Narima

Schott

Dichroic color effects glass

Narima® dichroic color effects glass from Schott has been developed to meet the increasing demand from architects and building owners for a glass that changes colors in different environments. Narima® colors vary depending on reflections, light conditions, the angle of view and the background.

Variable iridescent color effects are achieved by applying ultra-thin metal-oxide coatings to a range of base glasses. Each layer is applied in a thickness of less than 100 nanometers, and the resulting coating is hard, scratch resistant and extremely resistant to chemical attack. The combination of layers with high and low refractive indices results in a perceived color change.

Due to its unique and striking appearance, Narima® color effects glass opens up many new interior and exterior design possibilities and applications.

1-2. Different viewing angles and varying weather conditions result in a change of the color impression of NARIMA® color effects glass. Grand Canal Square 1, Dublin, Architect: Duffy Mitchell O'Donaghue (DMO'D)

SCHOTT North America, Inc.
555 Taxter Road
Elmsford, NY 10523
USA

www.us.schott.com
Tel: +1 914-831-2200
Fax: +1 914-831-2201

SCHOTT AG
Hattenbergstrasse 10
55122 Mainz
Germany

www.schott.com
Tel: +49 (0)6131-66-0
Fax: +49 (0)6131-66-2000

Artista® is a body-tinted colored, machine-drawn flat glass with a textured surface on one side. Artista® can be processed to produce both laminated glass and insulation glass. It can be thermally tempered beginning with a thickness of 4 mm in an unfused state.

Imera® is a non-textured, body-tinted, machine-drawn flat glass. Imera® is not only suited for use in expansive colored glass applications, but also in business premises – both inside and out. It also provides many individual design possibilities for adding attractive colored accents.

Imera® can be processed to produce both laminated safety glass and insulation glass. In thicknesses of 5 mm, 6 mm and 8 mm it can be thermally tempered.

1. Colorful expression for the visitors who pass the new staircase at SCHOTT in Mainz due to ARTISTA colored glass.

2. At the new head office of Novartis, for the very first time, there was a complete façade glazed with the colored glass Artista and Imera. In this application, the colored glass panes were used as a the outer building shell. To achieve the requested dimensions, the colored glass sheets were laminated onto or between two sheets of bigger sheets of white glass. This process is known as butt-glazing. Photo: C. Richters.

SCHOTT North America, Inc.
555 Taxter Road
Elmsford, NY 10523
USA

www.us.schott.com
Tel: +1 914-831-2200
Fax: +1 914-831-2201

SCHOTT AG
Hattenbergstrasse 10
55122 Mainz
Germany

www.schott.com
Tel: +49 (0)6131-66-0
Fax: +49 (0)6131-66-2000

The right lighting can make a significant impact on how comfortable we feel indoors. Using Opalika® by Schott, diffused lighting similar to a skylight with very little shadow can be created.

Unlike individual spotlights - of the type used in conventional illuminated ceilings –Opalika® distributes the light evenly, creating a pleasant atmosphere.

With the help of Opalika® white flashed opal glass, even "difficult" room conditions can be turned into unique celebrations. The white flashed opal glass has already become the embodiment of quality. This is a machine-drawn colorless base glass to which a thin layer of white flashed opal glass has been added that stands out in terms of how well it distributes light.

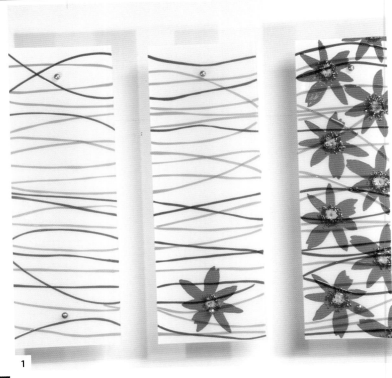

1

1. Decorative patterns on Opalika glass.

2. Foyer of the theater Mainz, Germany.

3. The special ceiling made out of OPALIKA creates an even lighting all over the room which puts the sculptures in perspective.

2

3

SCHOTT North America, Inc.
555 Taxter Road
Elmsford, NY 10523
USA

www.us.schott.com
Tel: +1 914-831-2200
Fax: +1 914-831-2201

SCHOTT AG
Hattenbergstrasse 10
55122 Mainz
Germany

www.schott.com
Tel: +49 (0)6131-66-0
Fax: +49 (0)6131-66-2000

Borosilicate glass is a high-quality, multi-functional float glass. Its wide range of outstanding product properties, such as its high thermal and chemical resistance, its excellent transparency and its good surface quality, allow access to new and high tech special glass applications.

On March 11th, 2007, the third anniversary of the terrorist attack in Madrid, a memorial was inaugurated at Atocha station in Madrid. The glassy monument consists of special glass bricks of the German Technology Group Scott. The bricks were made out of borosilicate glass at the plant in Grünenplan, Lower Saxony. Special borosilicate flat glass of the brand Borofloat which are produced in Jena, are the base of the roof construction for this special memorial.

1. Interior view of the memorial in Madrid.
2. Exterior of the memorial Photos: Jens Meyer.
3. Glass blocks made of borosilicate glass

SCHOTT North America, Inc.
555 Taxter Road
Elmsford, NY 10523
USA

www.us.schott.com
Tel: +1 914-831-2200
Fax: +1 914-831-2201

SCHOTT AG
Hattenbergstrasse 10
55122 Mainz
Germany

www.schott.com
Tel: +49 (0)6131-66-0
Fax: +49 (0)6131-66-2000

Polyvision

Polytronix

Electrochromic glass

At the flick of a switch, Polyvision™ glass becomes transparent from a dormant, cloudy-white translucent state. Polyvision™ Glass, therefore, provides creative design applications for architects and other innovative and practical users.

Opportunities for use in bath rooms/shower enclosures, private clinical areas, conference rooms, hospitals, exterior windows…etc. When the power is off, the liquid crystal molecules are randomly oriented so that incident light is scattered, and the Polyvision™ film is opaque. When electricity is applied, the liquid crystal molecules line up, the incident light passes through, and the Polyvision™ film is clear.

1. Glass turned off - translucent.
2. Glass turned on - transparent

Polytronix Inc.
805 Alpha Drive
Richardson, Texas 75081-2861
USA

www.polytronix.com
Tel: +1 972-238-7045
Fax: +1 972-644-0805
E-mail: sales@polytronix.com

AGC Flat Glass Europe has developed a new anti-bacterial glass that elimnates 99.9 % of bacteria and prevents the spreading of mold. It is ideal for hospitals, laboratories, educational centers, bathrooms, hotels, dining rooms, etc. AntiBacterial Glass eliminates microorganisms when they come in contact with the surface of the glass –in five seconds–, through an active ingredient based on silver. The ions interact and destroy the bacteria by deactivating its metabolism and altering its dividing mechanism.

AGC Flat Glass Europe Headquarters www.agc-flatglass.com
Chaussée de La Hulpe
1661170 Brussels
Belgium

Tel: +32 267-431-11
Fax: +32 267-244-62

DecorFlou

OmniDecor

High light transmission satin-finished glass

DecorFlou® satin-finished glass sheets feature strong light transmission with perfect diffusion. They therefore create a light that is unique – strong yet serene and immediately perceptible. Its innovative edge derives from OmniDecor® research: light transmission, filter, visual lightness, nuances, organic value, consistency in time. From separation panels to shelves, work-desks, closet doors, filing cabinets. Light - whether natural or artificial - passes through and illuminates environments without invading them. The boundary between architecture and design is only a matter of scale: noble materials preserve their value.

1. DecorFlou® Extraclear.
2. DecorFlou Anti-slip Treatment.
3. School Centre of industrial art, Lugano, Switzerland.
4. Fertin pharma building, Århus, Denmark.
5. Hotel Urthaler - Alpe di Siusi - Italy.
6. Hilton Hotel in Athens, Greece.

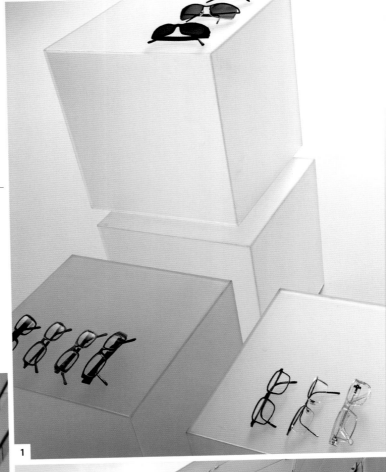

Omnidecor
via del Lavoro, 1
22036 Erba (CO)
Italy

www.omnidecor.net
Tel: +39 03-163-3701
Fax: +39 03-161-0331
E-mail: info@omnidecor.net

4

5

6

DecorFlou Design

OmniDecor

Textured satin-finished glass

Omnidecor® anticipates the most innovative interior design trends with its DecorFlou® Design new collection.

Besides Tree, Weed and Celsius decor from British designer Marc Krusin, and the three patterns Pisis, Quadrio, Rain and Daisy, the collection has been enriched with the new decor Blur, Beads, Laurel, Drops, Flow and Fuzzy from international designer Defne Koz. Designs in which harmonious lines extend over the glass surface without interruption to create ever-changing perspectives.

Elegant, eclectic, practical and strong, DecorFlou® is the perfect solution for a wide variety of applications in architecture and interior design: the glass surface is treated to let plenty of light through and produce unusual light effects while rendering the glass soft to the touch.

2

1

3

Omnidecor
via del Lavoro, 1
22036 Erba (CO)
Italy

www.omnidecor.net
Tel: +39 03-163-3701
Fax: +39 03-161-0331
E-mail: info@omnidecor.net

4

5

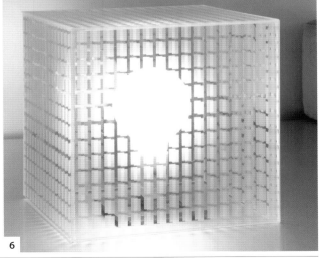

6

1. DecorFlou Design - Laurel decor by Defne Koz.
2. DecorFlou Design - Quadrio decor by Omnidecor.
3. DecorFlou Design - Mirror - Rain decor by Omnidecor.
4. DecorFlou Design - Fuzzy decor by Defne Koz.
5. DecorFlou Design - Tree decor by Marc Krusin.
6. DecorFlou Design - Blur decor by Defne Koz.

DecorGem Design

OmniDecor

Enamelled opaque and translucent glass sheets

Consistently committed to employing its expertise in the development of innovative products and more and more versatile applications, OmniDecor is now presenting its DecorGem Design collection.

The new line consists of glass sheets manufactured through a patented OmniDecor® technological process: colors are blended in the glass at high temperatures, along with highly distinctive patterns, either tone over tone – a dark background and smooth enamel surface –, or in an alternation between translucent and opaque – an acid-etched surface over a colored and polished background. The technique allows for wide-ranging creativity on a material platform perfectly suitable for both interior and exterior applications. Basic colors and a strong personality, the dynamic games of light and the alternating contrast between opaque and translucent, smooth and acid-etched, along with a vast choice of patterns, bring to life both interior environments and architectonic buildings. It takes full advantage of the surrounding light, which comes to the fore in an ever-changing dominance, remaining consistently at the edge of design and technology.

1. DecorGem Design - Weed decor by Marc Krusin - moonlight color.
2. DecorGem Design - Tree decor by Marc Krusin - sunset color.
3. DecorGem Design - Beads decor by Defne Koz - eclipse color.

Omnidecor
via del Lavoro, 1
22036 Erba (CO)
Italy

www.omnidecor.net
Tel: +39 03-163-3701
Fax: +39 03-161-0331
E-mail: info@omnidecor.net

The central theme of emdelight GmbH is to accentuate the architecture and to shape spaces by using artistic lighting concepts. Thomas Emde and emdelight bring architectural light projects (such as the illumination of the Commerzbank Tower in Frankfurt, the Tornado Tower and the Aspire Dome in Doha) to fruition artistically.

emdelight® glass germinated from such projects, and enables architects and designers to use glass as a new material with light and colors – literally – constructively.

emdelight® glass has the unique advantage that the illumination of glass façades becomes a feasible option and can be integrated into the façade. Furthermore emdelight® glass allows superior design of illuminated glass parapets, windows, public furniture, partition walls, ceiling elements, elevators, escalators, shower glass, shop interior exhibition booths and many more.

The special effect of the laminar illuminated emdelight®-glass (patent registered) is the result of the use of innovate LED technology and the individually designed dot matrix imprinted on the glass, which acts as "intended imperfection" diverting the light from the pane. The light is fed into the glass from one or two opposite edges. If RedGreenBlue (RGB) LED's are used, emdelight®-glass may illuminate in all colors of the RGB spectrum (arithmetically 16.7 million different possibilities). Harmonic light distribution all over the glass can be achieved. Special designs can be achieved by printing ornaments and fonts on the glass. The illuminated glass elements may be programmed and controlled pane by pane or all at once by a central control unit making interactive overall light design of the total area possible.

1. emdelight-glass façade with RGB Led's.
2. Spa wall with color changing emdelight-glass.
3. Shaped emdelight-glass.
4. High Bistro table, day and night.

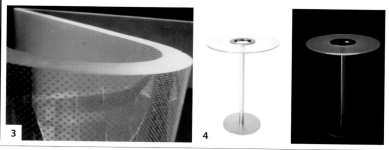

emdelight GmbH
Friedberger Landstr. 645
60389 Frankfurt a. M.
Germany

www.emdelight.com
Tel: +49 (0) 694-7 88-150
Fax: +49 (0) 694-7 88-1577
E-mail: info@emdelight.com

The Ginza collection was designed by Seves glassblock in collaboration with Renzo Piano for the Maison Hermès in Tokyo. Piano wanted 43 × 43 cm glass blocks for this project for the Tokyo headquarters of the French brand Hermès, as this was a scaled-down size of the French fashion house's famous square foulard (90 × 90 cm). It was an extraordinary size for this type of material and could not be found on the market. Piano also wanted the edges of the glass blocks to be mirror-varnished and the blocks to be installed very close to one another so as to form an almost uniform wall, without joints.

Seves accepted the challenge and after two years of experimentation set up a special line of production for a new type of square glass block with 42.8 cm sides, 12 cm thick and 16 kilograms in weight.

The parallel sides of the block have a smooth surface and a wavy surface, producing a ripple effect, like that of wind on water. The special design of the glass is further enhanced by the refraction of the sunlight, which is accentuated by the "mirror" treatment carried out on the blocks – the silvering of the surfaces along the whole of their width.

To enable the metallic supporting structure to be housed internally, without losing the sense of continuity between one block and another, the blocks are enclosed along their edges by the so-called "wings", which protrude 25 mm from the section.

The combination of the aforementioned properties, gives the wall a special silver mirror-like reflection with the visual elimination of the so-called "joint" between the blocks.

1

2

3

1. Maison Hermès in Ginza, Tokyo by Renzo Piano Building Workshop. External view
2. Maison Hermès internal view of the curved corner.
3. Maison Hermès, top floor.
4. The Q42 glass block, 42 × 42 cm.
5. The curved CURVE 24 block.

4

5

Seves S.p.a.
Via Reginaldo Giuliani, 360
50141, Firenze
Italy

www.sevesglassblock.com
Tel: +39 055-449-51
Fax: +39 055-45-52-95

Innovative, with a strong aesthetic impact, Pegasus, the top of the range Seves glass block, combines just the right balance in the search for formal perfection and high performance.

The result of technological solutions developed ad hoc to achieve large continuous glass surfaces without perceptible interruptions, Pegasus is more than a mere building element or an element of design.

Unlike conventional products, the Pegasus glass block has a distinctive protruding outer edge – the so-called "wings" – which makes it possible to adjust the size of the joint. This feature makes it possible to reduced the external thickness of the joint to as little as just 2 mm for the 19 × 19 × 8 cm size blocks and to 5 mm for larger blocks (such as those in the Ginza, Trapezoidal and Doric Collections). These measurements mean that it is possible to visually eliminate the perception of the joints and in this way create a homogeneous wall with a continuous surface, filling interior spaces with a light that is new and soft.

The Pegasus Metallizzato range offers the wavy glass design in 9 colors in addition to neutral, which is also available in the smooth glass design. All these products have a metallized finish as a result of a special system of mirroring along the inside of the edges of the glass blocks. This feature further accentuates the effect of continuity between one block and another, giving both the neutral and colored versions an attractive silvery appearance.

In order to satisfy the specific requirements for each application, Pegasus Metallizzato is available in a number of different formats, from the standard square 19 × 19 × 8 cm block to the rectangular 9.4 × 19 × 8 cm block, corner blocks and linear end or curved end blocks, which help to improve the aesthetic appearance of "all glass" surfaces.

1. **1.** The color range of the Pegasus Metallizzato collection.
2. **2-3.** Interior space with Pegasus Metallizzato glass blocks.
3. **4.** Rosa Modigliani Linear End Block.

Seves S.p.a.
Via Reginaldo Giuliani, 360
50141, Firenze
Italy

www.sevesglassblock.com
Tel: +39 055-449-51
Fax: +39 055-45-52-95

Mendini Collection

Seves - Atelier Mendini

Colored glass blocks

In the 1990s, Seves was the very first company to introduce color in glass blocks, thereby paving the way for new applications. Ten years later, Seves asked Atelier Mendini, an eclectically creative company, to further develop the use of color in glass blocks. This is how the Mendini Collection has come into being.

There are 16 colors in this range, from the boldest and sharpest ones to black and white, both in different degrees of transparency. And these vibrant colors, manufactured thanks to the "Pegasus" winged glass block technology (19 × 19 × 8 cm), smooth glass design and metallized finishing, shape a new generation of building elements for interiors. The handmade Mendini Collection blocks are colored using refined manufacturing technologies that preserve the purity of colors over time.

According to its creators, the Mendini Collection, with its shiny and youthful colors, has been designed to enable glass blocks to generate chromatic and figurative arrangements suited for elegant and refined combinations:

"The color alphabet of the Mendini Collection gives individually chosen colors, and their relationships and variations, the possibility to create endless chessboards of variants, from single colors up to kaleidoscopic effects. So far, sensuality, conceptuality, symbolism, hedonism and emotions are parameters that have been missing from the geometric language of glass blocks.

This collection opens up new poetic horizons that architects have not taken into account so far. However, they are now available and they are truly fascinating. New sparkling presences like sapphires, topazes, amber and ruby. And it is because of this rich appeal of nature that each color in this new collection has been given the expressive name of a precious stone."

1

4

2

3

Seves S.p.a.
Via Reginaldo Giuliani, 360
50141, Firenze
Italy

www.sevesglassblock.com
Tel: +39 055-449-51
Fax: +39 055-45-52-95

5

1. Interior space with Mendini glass blocks.
2. Mendini Collection, Zaffiro Q19 smooth metallized.
3. Mendini Collection, Corallo Q19 smooth metallized.
4. Seves glassblock Flagship Store in Milan, by Atelier Mendini. Photo: C. Lavatori.
5. The entire range of colors of the Mendini Collection.

Viewcol

Viewcol

High-resolution image lamination in glass

With modern architects increasingly incorporating glass into their designs, the urban landscape is being transformed. And, while glass imparts an open, airy feeling, is relatively inexpensive, durable, impervious to dirt and easy to maintain, it is a material that leaves little to the imagination, often appearing drab and commonplace. However, Viewcol, based in Sydney Australia, has come up with an intriguing and unprecedented answer to the bland glass façade and interior. Using PET foil, a polyester transparent 0.125-mm thick film, Viewcol has made it possible to laminate a unique, high-resolution image or picture in glass. Anything from illustrative logos, to luscious fruit and cascading waterfalls can be placed on the exterior or interior of a building changing the structure into a collage of bright and inviting colors and graphics.

In addition the laminated glass provides the benefit of strength and safety. Laminated glass was originally engineered for car windshields and security, bulletproof glass. While it is true that glass can break, the interlayer, the glue keeping the two glass plates together, prevents slivers from scattering.

Viewcol is produced both horizontally (landscape) and vertically (portrait), with a maximum width of 1450 mm. The length is unlimited, depending on the size of the lamination equipment. Viewcol is available in two qualities: Design – Premium 8000 and Design – Image 4000. Design – Image 4000 is mainly suited for large outdoor applications. The Design – Premium 8000 can produce a breathtaking reproduction of an image, until now considered impossible.

Viewcol brings brilliant color and imagery to the world of interior and exterior glass. Even solar panels can be emblazoned with stunning images.

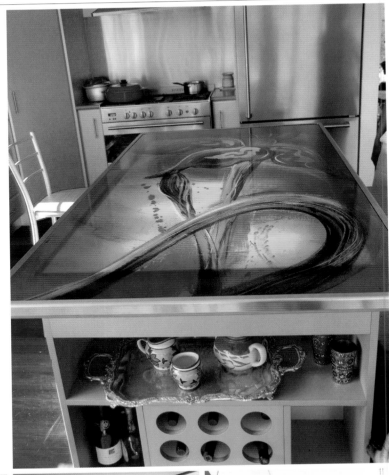

Viewcol Pty Ltd
Whites creek 33 – 35
Annandale 2038
Australia

www.viewcol.com
Tel.: +61 29-569-1700
Fax: +61 29-569-1400
E-mail: info@viewcol.com

SEFAR® Architecture Vision is a new woven textile made of special black monofilaments. The product range includes six basic fabrics with different mesh apertures from 25% up to 70%. All fabrics are coated on one side with a metal. Possible metals aare aluminum, chrome, copper, titanium, gold as well as an aluminum/copper combination that looks like brass. The metallic side is also printable with digital printing systems.

The fabric is normally laminated inside glass and can be used for several interior or exterior applications. Architects and designers are free to design on the front side with six different fabrics, six different metals and digital prints while the backside stays neutrally black and offers a lightly smoked view through.

Next to the design opportunities SEFAR® Architecture Vision also reduces solar heat gain and glare when it is used as a façade or roof element.

1. Vision glass, front side.
2. Vision glass, back side.
3. Macro photography of of two fabrics laminated in one glass.

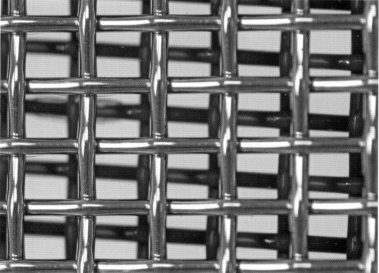

Sefar AG
Hinterbissaustrasse 12
CH-9410, Heiden
Switzerland

www.sefar.com
Tel: +41 71-898-5104
Fax: +41 71-898-5871
E-mail: vision@sefararchitecture.com

Nanogel

Cabot

Insulating silica aerogels

Nanogel is Cabot's trade name for its family of silica aerogels. Cabot is the only company to develop a commercialized process that allows for the production of aerogel material under ambient conditions. This process allows Cabot to control the material's porosity, pore size and distribution, and bypasses the high-cost traditional method of super-critical drying, so that Nanogel aerogel can be manufactured in a safe and continuous manner.

Aerogel used in fenestration products is an amorphous form of synthetic silica structured by nano-sized pores. About 95% of its volume is occupied by air, making aerogel the world's lightest solid material. The low solids content and extremely small pore size make it very effective against conduction and convection of heat. The amorphous silica particles are inherently safe under most construction material measurements. Additionally, aerogel is chemically and ultraviolet (UV)-stable, nontoxic, noncombustible, and generates no smoke. It is also permanently hydrophobic so it repels water, resists vapor migration, and does not support growth of mold or mildew spores. Aerogel is also permanently non-yellowing, with a luminous white appearance. Since silica is inert, aerogel can last the life of a structure and be recycled when the building is decommissioned.

Glazing systems incorporating Nanogel aerogel insulation can offer architects and building owners affordable and practical options in a variety of fenestration systems, satisfying both the relevant building codes and bringing diffuse light indoors.

1. Kitchen extension in south London. Original plans called for a large glazed roof. However, local authorities rejected this because it did not meet the UK energy-saving regulations which had become much more stringent. The owner set out to source a daylighting system with high insulation while still allowing the maximum amount of daylight in the small, restricted space.

2. Aerogel beads.

Cabot Corporation
Two Seaport Lane
Suite 1300
Boston, MA 02210
USA

www.cabot-corp.com
Tel: +1-617-345-0100
Fax: +1-617-342-6103

3-4. School extension in West London. Architects: Jacobs UK (Architecture) Ltd. Kalwall® light-diffusing insulated walls filled with Nanogel® aerogel were used on the south façade of the buildings to house additional classrooms, a new combined assembly hall/performance area, a dance studio, and an internet café & study area. Kalwall® panels filled with Nanogel offer thermal insulation four times better than insulating glass units, together with "museum" quality, diffuse glare- and shadow-free daylight.

5-6. Apartment building, Schwabing-Munich, Germany. Architects: Bauer & Steinert. This building is located in a busy street in the center of Munich, where noise was a real issue. The owner required the best possible thermal and acoustic insulation, as well as distinctive light diffusion. The products used were: Profilit™ glass and polycarbonate sheets filled with Nanogel.

TIMax enables a translucent glass façade to have excellent thermal insulation. It is made of very thin yarned glass fibers united with a light-stable binder. The air caught between the glass fibers acts as a very effective insulator. The light that comes through the material, although without some of its original intensity, preserves its color and creates a homogeneous illumination. Besides providing thermal insulation in winter, TIMax also controls solar radiation in summer and reduces heat gain.

1. Planning and enviroment department laboratory in Hamburg by MWP Architekten.
2. Pavillion in Graf-Wilhelm-Platz in Solingen by DBA Architekten.

Wacotech GmbH & Co.KG
Gewerbepark Brake
Querstraße 7
D-33729 Bielefeld
Germany

www.wacotech.de
Tel: +49 (0)521-962-0080
Fax: +49 (0)521-962-0089
E-mail: info@wacotech.de

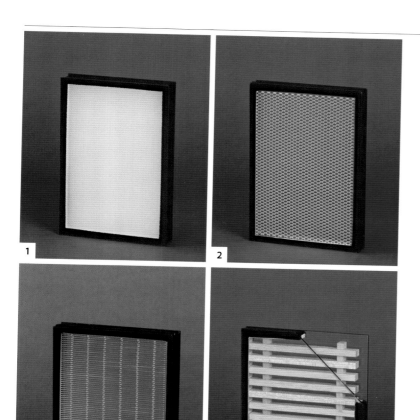

Okalux, which has its head office at Marktheidenfeld in Germany, manufactures innovative insulating glass solutions. The company provides unlimited possibilities for façade and roof design with a wide range of functional glasses and design-oriented glazing systems. Each product also gives the interior spaces unique character.

Okalux product development focuses on making optimum use of the daylight. Special inserts in the cavity between the panes have made it possible to harmonize the often conflicting requirements of protection and supply functionalities.

The versatility of Okalux products caters for a wide range of application possibilities. For example, the Okatech insulating glass panel with inserts made of expanded metal mesh or metal fabric is not only highly individual and aesthetically attractive but also functions as a directionally selective daylight system. The partially transparent glazing provides the inside of the building with soft room light and efficient protection from the sun and glare.

Okawood is a glass panel with a filigree wooden grid in the cavity between the panes. The wooden louvers function as a shield from the sun and dazzle while allowing warm, daylight tones to fall into the room.

Okagel offers the optimum use of daylight and maximum energy efficiency. A translucent Nanogel® in the cavity between panes provides for positive physical properties. The façade element therefore fulfils the highest requirements for thermal insulation, light diffusion and sound and glare protection.

1. OKA*GEL* with Nanogel© filling.
2. OKA*TECH* with expanded metal insert.
3. OKA*TECH* with wire mesh.
4. OKA*WOOD* with timber grid.
5. Detail of Okagel.

OKALUX GmbH
Am Jöspershecklein 1
97828 Marktheidenfeld
Germany

www.okalux.com
Tel: +49 (0) 9391 900-0
Fax: +49 (0) 9391 900-100
E-mail: info@okalux.de

Glamour, Aureo

Trend

Glass mosaic tiles

The charm of the hand crafting of glass and its transparency characterize Glamour, the glass tesserae mosaic by Trend. This collection, enhanced by its wide color range, is available in two versions: plain color and grained, made through mixing the glass with avventurina, a stone giving preciousness to the glass surface. The glass tesserae are available in various sizes and their 1 cm thickness makes them highly durable. Glamour is ideal for both monochrome creations or personalized solutions and any kind of application: floor and wall coverings, indoor and outdoor environments.

Aureo is the unique and unrepeatable history of an art craft that has handed down mysterious alchemies for generations and has revived the old crafts of Byzantine gold leaf. The glass mosaic, hand crafted with a very fine 24 carat gold leaf, is available in three sizes and many different hues for innumerable possibilities of expression.

1

1. Salviati boutique, New York, USA. Architect: Paola Navone. Floor: Glamour collection, 10 × 10 cm.
2. Hotel Urban, Madrid, Spain. Wall: Aureo collection, 2 × 2 cm.
3. Hotel Granados 83, Barcelona, Spain. Wall: Glamour collection, 5 × 5 cm.

2

3

TREND GROUP S.p.A.
Piazzale Fraccon, 8
36100 Vicenza
Italy

www.trend-vi.com
Tel: +39 044-433-8711
Fax: +39 044-473-8747
E-mail: info@trend-vi.com

Blazestone tiles are crafted entirely from post-industrial and post-consumer glass without any addition of oxides or colorants. Each tile is handmade from unique combinations of glass that give the tiles their distinctive appearance and subtle color variation. Therefore, each tile is unique and there are slight differences in shape and variations in the surface. These features are part of the beauty and special character of Blazestone Tile.

Bedrock Industries
1 401 W. Garfield Street
Seattle, WA 98119
USA

www.bedrockindustries.com
Tel: +1-877-283-7625
Fax: +1-206-283-0497
E-mail: info@ bedrockindustries.com

Fashionglass

Bluestein

Decorative glass floor

Immagination and emotion are the ingredients at the base of this glamour line. Fashionglass is a modern reappraisal of Baroque style. This product is characterized by versatile applications; it may be used for coverings, raised or floating floorings, stairs and decorations.

Fashionglass contains fragments of colored and neutral glass, which attain their best expressive capacity becoming real jewels.

Bluestein S.R.L.
Viale Roma, 26
24011 Alme' (BG)
Italy

www.bluestein.it
Tel: +39 (0)35-637-952
Fax: +39 (0)35-547-1267
E-mail: info@bluestein.it

Metals such as copper and brass have been utilized by Bluestein to realize floorings with a strong and lasting surface. It has been realized by stratifing the metal base with extralight glass. Metal-glass tiles do not oxidize. Copper, brass and steel have been used in Metalglass. Bluestein works all these metals by hand, giving to the surfaces a special decoration. It may be soft or strong and the metal's color remains unaltered over time. Metalglass can be used for floorings, raised floorings, coverings tops, stairs and interior decorations.

Bluestein S.R.L.
Viale Roma, 26
24011 Alme' (BG)
Italy

www.bluestein.it
Tel: +39 (0)35-637-952
Fax: +39 (0)35-547-1267
E-mail: info@bluestein.it

Plastics

Although plastics are the most recent members of the family of architectural materials, they have become one of the most popular. Many different types of plastic are available as well as plastic-mineral mixtures like Corian and Hi-Macs. Although plastics can be relatively easily formed into almost any shape, the commercially available products are usually in the form of sheets. Honeycomb sheets are a common and very effective type of plastic (or composite) sheet offering high durability for low weight. Ecological concerns have become important in the field of plastics. Thermoplastics are recyclable but the practice is not yet widespread. Some companies offer products where the "defects" of recycled plastic become aesthetic qualities making its use not only a practical issue but also a statement. The use of cellulose as a carbon source instead of petrol is another way of creating plastics with lower environmental impact. "Smart" polymers with shape-memory or thermochromic abilities are also used in interior design elements.

Plastics used in construction

Name	Abbreviation	Common names	Softening temperature	Melting point	Density (kg/m³)
Polyamide	PA	Nylon®, Rilsan®	50°C	220-260°C	
Polycarbonate	PC		140-150°C	230-250°C	1200-1220
Polyethylene	PE		35-50°C	120-135°C	
Polyethylene Terephthalate	PET		73°C	255°C	1455
Polymethyl Methacrylate	PMMA	acrylic, Plexiglas®	110-130°C	210-240°C	1190
Polypropylene	PP	Tyvek®		165-170°C	855
Polystyrene	PS		90°C	180°C	
Polytetrafluorethylene	PTFE	Teflon®		327°C	2200
Polyvinyl Chloride	PVC	PVC	70-100°C	140-170°C	1390

Plastics

Smile Plastics

Smile Plastics

Plastic sheets from recycled objects

Smile Plastics is committed to sourcing and developing innovative ideas and markets for sheets made from recycled plastics waste. Smile Plastics sheets have been used extensively all over the world as furniture, shop fittings, work surfaces, bath panels, and screens, etc., in domestic, commercial and office environments.

In 1994 a range of sheets made from old plastics bottles was launched. The bottles are collected, sorted, flaked and thoroughly washed to remove any remaining contaminants. Like multi-colored cornflakes the pieces are compressed into sheets which retain all the riotous colors of the original bottles. In 2002 and 2003 new products were launched, made from crushed CDs and plastic water bottles, banknotes, and Dapple, and since then some of our funkiest sheets have been made from old Mobile Phones and Kids Wellies.

The CD range consists of a rigid, sparkly sheet made from crushed CDs suspended in a transparent blue plastic. The blue was originally the large plastic bottles that dispense cold drinking water in offices and the crushed CDs include illicit ones seized and destroyed by Trading Standards Officers. Made from polycarbonate, the sheets are tough and rigid yet warm to the touch.

The Mobiles range uses some of the 15 million UK mobiles that get discarded each year.

1. The Bottles sheets used as toilet cladding.
2. Furniture by IWI Green made from Mobiles.
3. Detail of the Mobiles sheet texture.
4. Aaron Moore Furniture, ESC Chaise from CD sheet.
5. Dalby Visitor Centre, toilet cubicles made with Dapple sheets.
6. Table from Bottles sheet designed by NaughtOne.
7. The CD sheet used in a bar interior by Mark Lintott Design.
8. Reception desk from Mobiles sheet.

Smile Plastics
Mansion House
Ford, Shrewsbury, SY5 9LZ
UK

www.smile-plastics.co.uk
Tel: +44 (0) 170-450-9888
Fax: +44 (0) 170-450-9777
E-mail: sales@smile-plastics.co.uk

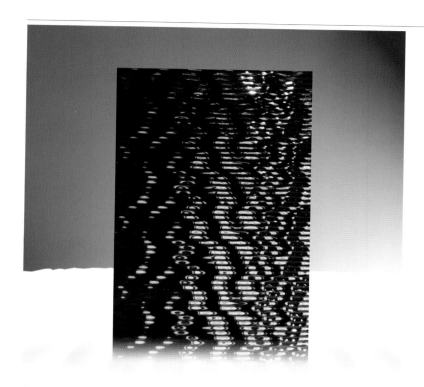

R-Cast™ Textures is an acrylic or resin panel with deep sculpted customized patterns. The versatility of R-Cast™ Textures allows it to pair well with lighting or simply stand alone without any special illumination. When illuminated, the textures carved into the panel take on a new dimension of depth in design while the lighting dances off the various curves. Without any special illumination, the textured panels reflect available ambient lighting to produce shadows that create depth.

R-Cast™ Textures can be customized to suit any project needs and is available in solid opaque colors, as well as clear and unlimited translucent custom colors as part of the R-Cast™ Palette product line. R-Cast™ Textures can also utilize the fire-rated R-Cast™ Dura in both the white opaque and black opaque colors.

A benefit in using R-Cast™ acrylic in interior design is that it weighs only half as much as glass but is seventeen times stronger than it and four times stronger than concrete. The optical clarity of the base acrylic material ensures that when the textures are carved into the panel, they reflect the precise effects required of them.

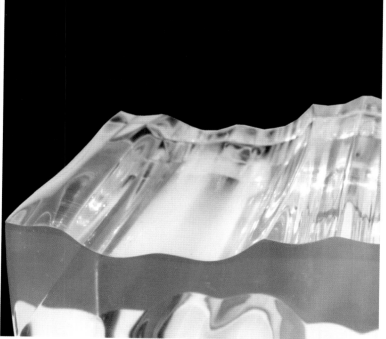

Reynolds Polymer Technology
607 Hollingsworth St.
Grand Junction, CO 81505
USA

www.reynoldspolymer.com
Tel: +1 970-241-4700
Fax: +1 970-241-4747
E-mail: CustomerService@ReynoldsPolymer.com

R-Cast Ice

Reynolds Polymer Technology, Inc.

Acrylic panel with randomized ice texture

The debut of R-Cast™ Ice in a martini bar in Bucharest continues to make waves with architects and designers. Reynolds Polymer Technology, Inc. is one of the first acrylic manufacturers to perfect the texture so that it not only looks realistic, but its surface texture also feels realistic – and without the freezing temperatures.

Formed out of the R-Cast™ Acrylic product line, the texture of the ice is completely randomized without any repetitive patterns. This ensures that the acrylic Ice more closely resembles real ice, particularly with light refractions off the surface.

R-Cast™ Ice is ideal for use within the hospitality and entertainment markets, particularly for decorative paneling, partitions, water features, signage, furniture, or other displays. Each sheet of ice is truly one-of-a-kind, formable and can have a phenomenal impact with special lighting effects, making it perfect for projects like restaurants, hotels, or nightclubs.

By using a variety of different translucencies and hundreds of colors that are available, and with a creative use of lighting, innumerable effects can be created with R-Cast™ Ice. Available in 12.7 mm and 25.4 mm thicknesses, R-Cast™ Ice is available in sheets as large as 1.2 × 2.4 m, which can be fabricated or formed into a variety of shapes for custom projects.

Reynolds Polymer Technology
607 Hollingsworth St.
Grand Junction, CO 81505
USA

www.reynoldspolymer.com
Tel: +1 970-241-4700
Fax: +1 970-241-4747
E-mail: CustomerService@ReynoldsPolymer.com

R-Cast™ Mirage and R-Cast™ Palette share similar technology in producing custom acrylic and resin-based panels for interiors. Using proprietary fabrication methods, custom colors, images, or graphics can be flawlessly reproduced on acrylic or resin-based materials to create sophisticated interior environments.

R-Cast™ Mirage and R-Cast™ Palette benefit tremendously from illumination and the visual appearance of the panel can be altered simply by changing or removing the lighting. Both products promise to give architects and designers greater flexibility in designing with resins as the ability to provide custom colors to match furniture, lighting, and décor, or to create custom graphics that fall into the designer's theme create endless design options.

R-Cast™ Mirage has a number of library images following nature, industrial, and abstract themes, while R-Cast™ Palette has 120 colors in the library. Customization of both of these products ensures that designers can achieve precisely the look they desire. Available materials include white opaque, white translucent, or clear acrylic and the fire-rated R-Cast™ Dura in white opaque.

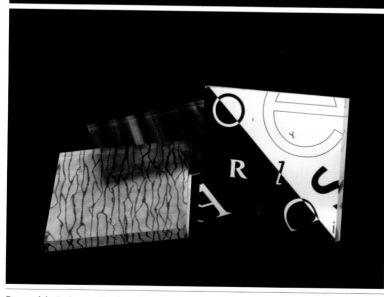

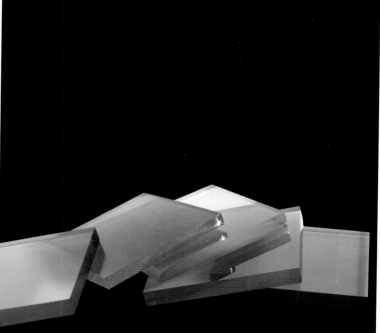

Reynolds Polymer Technology
607 Hollingsworth St.
Grand Junction, CO 81505
USA

www.reynoldspolymer.com
Tel: +1 970-241-4700
Fax: +1 970-241-4747
E-mail: CustomerService@ReynoldsPolymer.com

Starlight is a composite panel with inner patented macro-cellular translucent SAN core bonded with external layers in acrylic offered in various finishes and standard colors.

Thanks to its characteristics of lightweight, stiffness, translucency and unique aesthetical feature resulting from the geometrical pattern of its core, this structural panel has a wide variety of indoor applications. Easy to cut, Starlight panel can be finished with standard accessories profiles and systems such as frames, handles, hinges. Starlight can also be edged with the same material used for the external layers.

Lightben is an ultra-light composite panel produced bonding a core made of Polycarbonate transparent cylinders to external layers in acrylic in various finishes and several standard colours. The Lightben's particular core structure creates a partial transparency which varies according to the visual angle, while the external layers allow a variation in transmittance and color shading of the light.

Thanks to these special aesthetical features and an outstanding lightweight and stiffness, Lightben is suitable for a wide variety of indoor applications. Easy to cut Lightben panels can be finished with standard accessories profiles and systems such as frames, handles, hinges. Lightben can also be edged with the same material used for the external layers.

1

2

1-2. Applications of the Starlight panel.
3. Lightben panel.
4. Starlight panel.

3

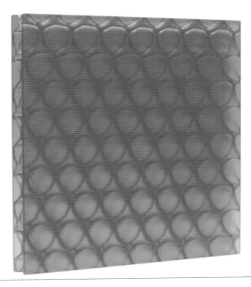

4

Bencore Srl
Via S. Colombano 9
54100 Massa (MS)
Italy

www.bencore.it
Tel: +39 058-583-0129
Fax: +39 058-583-5167
E-mail: info@bencore.it

Based on a unique core production process and a highly developed bonding technology Design Composite GmbH manufactures a broad variety of three-layer plastic panels. Among the best technical product characteristics the excellent translucency opens a wide range of applications for modern design. Natural as well as artificial light sources create the perfect frame for the panels.

The clear-PEP® and AIR-board® lines are for interior use (partitions, wall cladding, floors, ceilings) shop design, booth and design furniture constructions. Due to the excellent stiffness, the high impact resistance, the low weight, the UV resistance and the outstanding light refraction effects, the clear-PEP® panels are perfect materials for innovative design in architecture.

Design Composite GmbH
Klausgasse 32
A-5730 Mittersill
Austria

www.design-composite.com
Tel: +43 (0) 656-240-6090
Fax: +43 (0) 656-240-6090-09
E-mail: info@design-composite.at

ViewPan® PMMA

Wacotech

Translucent honeycomb panels

ViewPan PMMA is a decorative honeycomb composite panel with a unique patented PET core and acrylic (PMMA) faces. The honeycomb structure provides great strength and light weight while it also creates stunning visual effects. Wacotech offers an extensive choice of colors with either glossy or frosted ('Softtone') surfaces and a range of thicknesses, between 19 and 80 mm, that can be manufactured to suit specific framing systems. Sealed edges are also possible to make upon request.

ViewPan has a great range of uses in interior design: screens, partitions, doors, ceiling panels, fascias, illuminated walls, displays, furniture and shelving are some of the possibilities.

Wacotech GmbH & Co.KG
Gewerbepark Brake
Querstraße 7
D-33729 Bielefeld
Germany

www.wacotech.de
Tel: +49 (0)521-962-0080
Fax: +49 (0)521-962-0089
E-mail: info@wacotech.de

ViewPan PET is a decorative honeycomb composite panel with a unique patented PET core and PET faces. ViewPan PET is flame retardant & self extinguishing. For ViewPan PET Wacotech offers the same range thicknesses as for ViewPan PMMA.

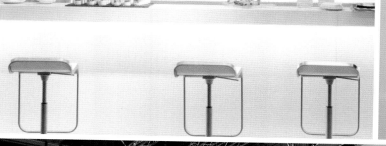

Wacotech GmbH & Co.KG
Gewerbepark Brake
Querstraße 7
D-33729 Bielefeld
Germany

www.wacotech.de
Tel: +49 (0)521-962-0080
Fax: +49 (0)521-962-0089
E-mail: info@wacotech.de

B-Clear

Mykon

Honeycomb/Glass Sandwich Panels

Constructed with an aluminum honeycomb core and sandwiched between polycarbonate or glass skins; this strong, rigid, yet light-weight structure is ideal for partitioning. The visual fish-eye effect is achieved through the unique bonding of the polycarbonate or glass to the aluminum honeycomb, producing a unique effect that not only allows the room to be flooded with light but also ensures privacy. Each individual cell allows light to pass through it but together the cells remain translucent. As a result, when placed in direct sunlight or artificial light, the panel appears to sparkle. The hand-made design yields an individual quality to each panel, making every partition unique.

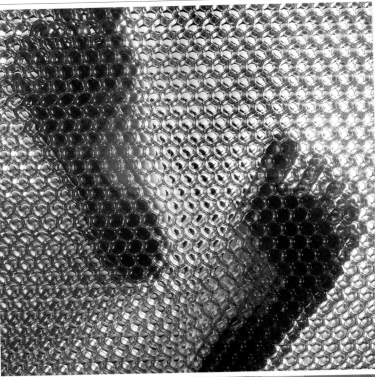

Mykon
5 Stukeley Business Centre
Blackstone Road
Huntingdon, Cambridgeshire, PE29 6EF
United Kingdom

www.mykon-systems.com
Tel: +44 (0) 148-041-5070
E-mail: sales@mykon-systems.com

Soft Gem is one of many products designed by Fabrice Covelli that are made with a technology that encapsulates urethane gel inside a strong flexible urethane skin. Soft Gem is a highly tactile material made from the juxtaposition of myriad colorful semispherical pads that create a vibrant and mesmerizing panel, especially when illuminated with light. Originally, Soft Gem was designed as malleable semi-precious stones to be mounted onto jewelry; however, it has also been applied to interior doors, decorative partitions, bed headboards, and floor and table lamps.

Fproduct, Inc - Fabrice Covelli
250 Saint Marks Avenue
Brooklyn NY 11238
USA

www.fproduct.net
Tel: +1 917-202-2349
E-mail: getinfo@fproduct.net

Lumicor

Lumicor

Recycled resin panels with embedded objects

Lumicor allows architects and designers to create memorable spaces with these eco-friendly architectural resin panels encapsulated with texture and color. The aesthetic and functional products offer endless possibilities for simple and practical ways to bring light, texture, color, and inspiration to any space. Utilizing this patented technology, Lumicor creates eco-friendly resin panels using recycled resin and sustainable materials, including organics from nature, metals, fabrics, color infusion, and the firm's own unique designs. Lumicor panels are offered in acrylic and additional specialized resin options to suit applications. In addition, Lumicor supports customers' projects with a hardware assortment, cutting, and fabrication services. Lumicor offers all its products in R4® materials including Mixed Bottles™, winner of Neocon Gold in 2008.

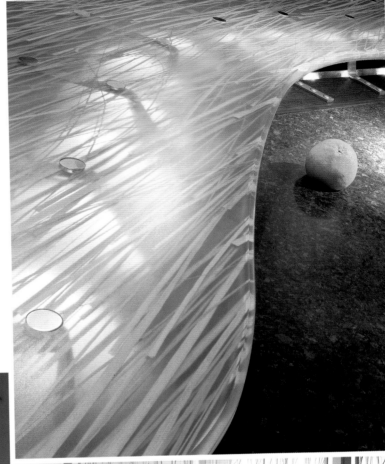

Lumicor
1400 Monster Road SW
Renton, WA 98057
USA

www.lumicor.com
Tel: +1 425-255-4000
Fax: +1 425-277-1872
E-mail: sales@lumicor.com

Aire Pad

Fabrice Covelli

Rubber and silicon cushioned panels

Aire Pad was developed by designer Fabrice Covelli, which applies the Fproduct gel encapsulation technology to non-compressed air trapped within a strong flexible skin.

The enclosed air provides a very efficient and comfortable cushioning effect while the flexible skin, built at the desired shape will retain its perfectly sleek appearance after pressure is released. The products made with this technology are lighter, faster to produce, and less expensive than gel-filled items.

Rubber and silicon may be equally used for applications such as wall tiles and panels, cushions and furniture.

The color, mold pattern and embossed design may be customized. The material is UV resistant, waterproof and has good shock and sound absorption.

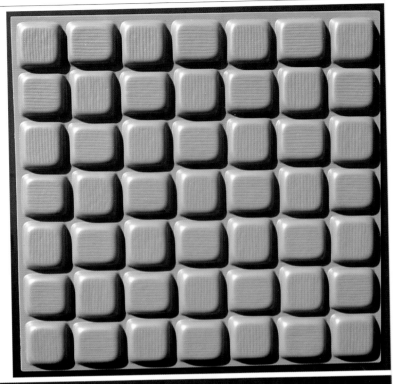

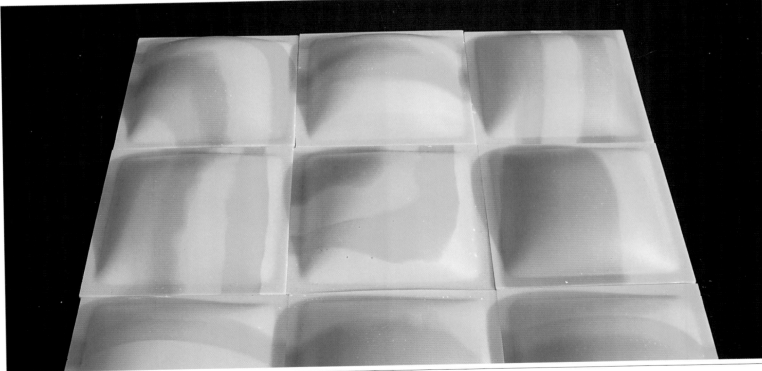

Fproduct, Inc - Fabrice Covelli
250 Saint Marks Avenue
Brooklyn NY 11238
USA

www.fproduct.net
Tel: +1 917-202-2349
E-mail: getinfo@fproduct.net

1

The DuPont™ Tyvek® family of membranes offers protection during construction and over the life of a building. They consist of extremely durable lightweight flexible sheet materials manufactured from spunbonded polyolefin. Tyvek® is suitable for use as breather membranes in pitched roof construction, most forms of timber and metal frame walls, and can be used in new-build, refurbishment and extension projects.

Tyvek® HomeWrap® helps protect a home like a windbreaker; stopping the wind and rain penetration by forming a protective skin around the house. It is breathable, allowing incidental moisture vapor to escape, thereby helping to prevent moisture build-up which can lead to costly water damage.

Tyvek® AtticWrap™ creates a sealed attic system that helps reduce dynamic air leakage and energy loss through a fully vented roof. Moisture vapor passes through AtticWrap™ helping to prevent moisture build-up which could lead to the formation of mold, mildew and wood rot. AtticWrap™ is layered with a unique, metallized material that creates a low-emissivity (low-e) surface which helps improve the overall heating and cooling efficiency for the building. When fully integrated, AtticWrap™ acts as a secondary weather barrier, helping block water infiltration into the attic through the soffits and air vents by allowing the water to drain back outside the building more efficiently.

1. Tyvek® façade diagram. The structure of the ventilated facade incorporating Tyvek® adopted in premium apartment complex in the Sokolniki district. Tyvek® is used as an underlay on top of mineral wool.

2. Tyvek® Weather Barrier Systems used by Yellowstone National Park.

3. Tyvek® HomeWrap™ micrograph. The microscopic pores in Tyvek® help protect homes and commercial structures from the elements.

All images: Courtesy of DuPont.

DuPont™ and Tyvek® are a trademark and a registered trademark of E. I. du Pont de Nemours and Company or its affiliates.

2

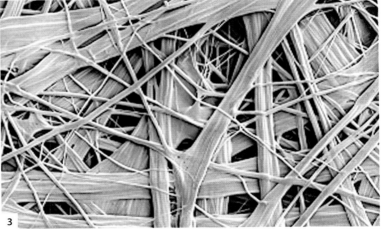

3

www.buildingonscience.dupont.com

Nano Vent-skin

Agustin Otegui

Energy-generating building skin

Nano Vent-skin is a set of micro turbines (25 × 10,8 mm), which generate energy from wind and sunlight.

The outer skin of the structure absorbs sunlight through an organic photovoltaic skin and transfers it to the nano-fibers inside the nano-wires which then is sent to the storage units located at the end of each panel. Each turbine generates energy by chemical reactions on each end where it makes contact with the nano-wires. The outer skin of the nano-wires has polarized organisms which are responsible for this process on every turbine's turn. The inner skin of the turbine's blades works as a filter absorbing CO_2 from the environment as wind passes through them.

Each panel has four round supply units (one on each corner). These units are in charge of:

- Monitoring that all the turbines are working.
- Delivering material to regenerate broken or malfunctioning turbines.
- Receiving and storing the energy produced by the turbines.

The fact of using nano-bioengineering and nano-manufacturing as a means of production is to achieve an efficient zero emission material which uses the right kind and amount of material where needed.

These micro organisms have not been genetically altered; they work as a trained colony where each member has a specific task in this symbiotic process. For example, an ant or a bee colony, where the queen knows what has to be done and distributes the tasks between the members.

NVS is like the human skin. When we suffer a cut, our brain sends signals and resources to this specific region to get it restored as soon as possible.

NVS works in the same way. Every panel has a sensor on each corner with a material reservoir. When one of the turbines has a failure or breaks, a signal is sent through the nano-wires to the central system and building material (micro organisms) is sent through the central tube in order to regenerate this area with a self assembly process.

In order to achieve the best outcome of energy, the blades of each turbine are symmetrically designed. With this feature, even if the wind's direction changes, each turbine adapts itself by rotating clockwise or anti-clockwise, depending on the situation.

www.agustin-otegui.com
nanoventskin.blogspot.com
E-mail: agustinotegui@gmail.com
Tel: +52-55-4439-9655

Fassawall is a colored façade foil that is applied behind glass, semi-transparent or open façades. Because the foil is placed a number of centimetres behind the façade plates, the product adds an effect of depth to the façade. Fassawall is a damp-open foil, water resistant, UV resistant, fire retardant, durable, color true, flexible and therefore easy to work with. These properties make the use of an underlying foil layer unnecessary. It is available in any RAL color and therefore offers many possibilities.

Fassawall BV
Po Box 338
7200 AH Zutphen
The Netherlands

www.fassawall.com
Tel: +31 (0) 57-551-8310
Fax: +31 (0) 57-551-1538
E-mail: info@fassawall.com

At the core of Konarka's technology is its active photovoltaic material that is made from semi-conducting polymers and nano-engineered materials. The printed active material absorbs photons to trigger the release of electrons which are then transported to create electricity. The active material is sandwiched between printed electrodes which are sandwiched between the substrate and the transparent packaging material. The finished product is only 2-10 mm (50-250 μm) thick.

Konarka's technology enables integration into multiple application channels including portable devices, such as mobile phones, PDAs, digital music players, and laptops; architectural materials, such as rooftops, sidings, window panes, blinds, and awnings; sensor networks; and fabrics, such as jackets and handbags that can charge portable devices.

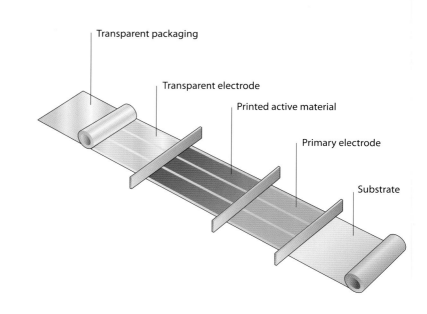

Transparent packaging

Transparent electrode

Printed active material

Primary electrode

Substrate

Konarka Technologies, Inc.
116 John Street
Suite 12, 3rd Floor
Lowell, MA 01852
USA

www.konarka.com
Tel: +1 978-569-1400
Fax: +1 978-569-1402

1

2

3

4

Gobbetto's activity is devoted to developing high technology systems and techniques to obtain surfaces and backgrounds, capable of highlighting contents and artistic and communicative languages, expressed through the plasticity of resin materials.

Dega Art is a resin floor that offers seamless surfaces obtained with mixed techniques and assorted inserted decorations.

The aesthetical effects are done by hand, in a wide range of colors - bright, matt and satin finish. The medium thickness is 2-3 mm. Dega Art has good features of resistance to wear and foot traffic and is easy to clean. It is suitable for residences, offices or showrooms.

Dega Art Spatulated is a spatula-applied resin floor and coating with the use of traditional techniques, suitable for seamless surfaces with spatulated effects, highlighted to greater or lesser extents. Dega Art Spatulated shows good features of resistance to wear and foot traffic.

5

6

1-4. Aplications of Dega Art.
5-6. Aplications of Dega Art Spatulated.
7-12. Examples of Dega Art textures.

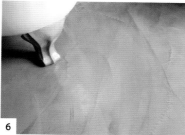

7

8

9

10

11

12

Gobbetto S.r.l.
via Carroccio, 16
Milano
Italy

www.gobbetto.it
Tel: +39 028-322-269
Fax: +39 028-940-4269
E-mail: gobbetto@gobbetto.com

UPM ProFi Deck

UPM

Wood plastic composite decking

UPM ProFi Deck is a new type of composite material manufactured from recycled paper and plastic which is surplus from UPM's label stock production. As there is no other significant recycling process for the label surplus material, the manufacture of UPM ProFi Deck actually reduces land-fill and waste incineration.

Stylish, durable and requiring low maintenance, UPM ProFi Deck is an ideal solution for outdoor use in garden decks, patios, terrace areas, marinas and boardwalks, as well as many other challenging applications. UPM ProFi is developed to sustain all kinds of weather, wear and UV light. Yet it feels natural to touch and is easy to install.

The main advantages of UPM ProFi Deck are design alternatives and creativity. Seven fresh colors offer the possibility to create patterns, shapes, and contors. Unlike other wood-based wood plastic composites, UPM ProFi is virtually lignin free. This gives it better natural resistance to the "greying" process caused by ultra violet light.

UPM ProFi Deck is an archtype of low maintenance product. There is no need for surface treatment, only periodical cleaning with jet hose or a normal hose and brush is recommended. The decking has an exceedingly hardwearing surface and yet it still feels comfortable and natural to the touch. Being splinterfree, it is ideal for bare feet. UPM ProFi has a high-friction surface and very good anti-slip properties, which make it a safe platform, even when wet. With a surface that is not wire-brushed, UPM ProFi Deck's low moisture absorption has a higher natural resistance to stains, mould and warping.

UPM ProFi does not contain any harmful chemicals and can be thereby recycled or disposed of with normal household waste.

1

2

UPM
Eteläesplanadi 2
P.O. Box 380
FI-00101 Helsinki
Finland

www.upm-kymmene.com
Tel: +358 (0) 20-415-111
Fax: +358 (0) 20-415-110
E-mail: info@upm-kymmene.com

1. UPM ProFi Deck sample colors.
2. The raw material for ProFi.
3. House in Kangasala, Finland.
4. House in Vaasa, Finland.
5. UPM ProFi Deck Deck construction system.
6. House in Pori, Finland.

Geo

Sturm und Plastic - Gigi Rigamonti

Clear plastic elements for interiors

The Geo system is composed of clear plastic elements that are rectangular and angled and semicircular ones of various radii that can be combined to form interior dividers and elements.
The Geo Bricks are joined together by a ring component, while the Geo Geo elements are fixed together using clear silicone.

1. Geo Bed, an application of the Geo system.
2-3. Walls from Geo Brick.
4-5. Geo Geo elements.
6. Geo Brick.

Sturm und Plastic
Via Coti Zelati 90
20030 Palazzolo Milanese, Milan
Italy

www.sturmundplastic.com
Tel: +39 029-904-4222
Fax: +39 029-904-5611
E-mail: info@sturmundplastic.com

Face is a polyvalent system that offers multiple solutions: the flexibility of the product is translated into innumerable configurations such as counters, desks, separation walls or shelving systems.

Sturm und Plastic
Via Coti Zelati 90
20030 Palazzolo Milanese, Milan
Italy

www.sturmundplastic.com
Tel: +39 029-904-4222
Fax: +39 029-904-5611
E-mail: info@sturmundplastic.com

Diamond chair

Nendo

Chair from the diamond atomic structure

The dense and atomic structure of a diamond efficiently disperses strength and light throughout the material, giving diamonds their singular hardness and shine. The Diamond chair is a "strong but flexible" structure that uses this atomic array as a motif and responds to pressure by absorbing rather than resisting it, and has the suppleness of human organs or muscles.

Nendo created such a structure through powder sintering rapid prototyping technology that uses a laser to transform polyamide particles into a hard mold based on 3D CAD data. The RP technology allows added thickness where users need support, and to carve away the material into a thinner, more flexible and responsive thickness in places where users want comfort, allowing one material to serve multiple purposes. There is a limit to the size of an object an RP machine can produce, so the chair was designed in two pieces that snap together like a puzzle, and are attached after each piece had hardened. Since the pieces are cast at the same time, the problem of parts not fitting together exactly during assembly is eliminated, because any shrinkage or distortion due to heat occurs at the same time and the same rate.

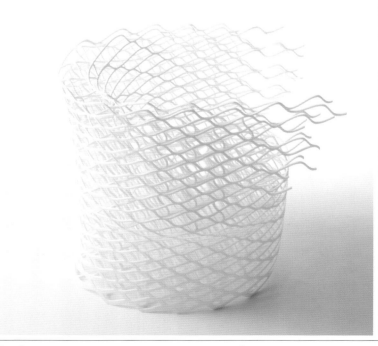

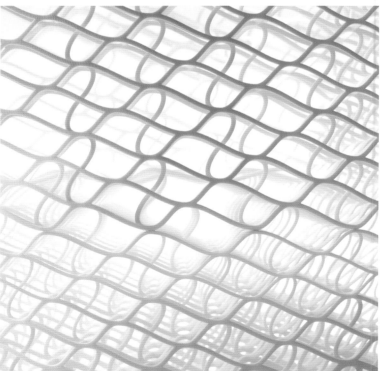

Nendo
2-2-16-5F Shimomeguro Meguro-ku
Tokyo 153-0064
Japan

www.nendo.jp
Tel: +81 (0) 36-661-3750
Fax: +81 (0) 36-661-3751
E-mail: info@nendo.jp

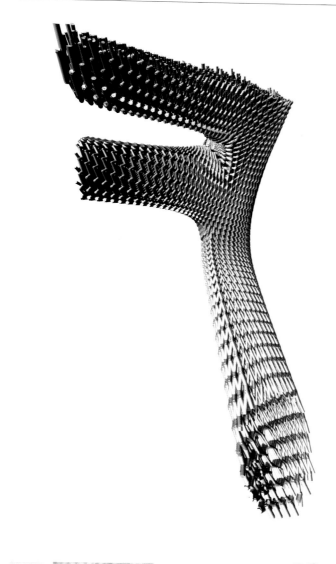

Based on an analogy with the highly efficient cellular structure of living wood or bone, which adapts to its environment as it grows, the chair's interior is comprised of a fine lattice that minimizes weight while maximizing strength. The design method combines principles of evolution and artificial intelligence to create a material that responds to its environment by growing denser in the areas required to best withstand the external forces applied when the chair is in use.

The composition of the cells is the result of a computational process directly modeled on nature that creates a modular space frame structure of tiny interconnected struts, specifically suited to the material and fabrication process. A genetic algorithm, using the principles of natural evolution, has been used to generate the topology of the structural cells. Using machine learning techniques each one is given just enough intelligence to reorient itself or change its shape, size or structure depending on where it sits in the body of the chair. A section through the vertical leg of the chair, for example, reveals cells with a greater density toward the surface to counter the higher tensile or compressive stresses that result as it bends.

www.vr.ucl.ac.uk/people/sean/
E-mail: s.hanna@ucl.ac.uk

Introduced in 1998, ECOsurfaces products provide long wearing recycled rubber flooring to the educational, healthcare, retail, hospitality, institutional and fitness markets, among others. For more than a decade, the line has earned a reputation for durable surfacing that is as comfortable to walk on as it is fashionable, thanks to a selection of patterns and colors that make a unique design statement.

Its low life cycle costs and ease of maintenance have made ECOsurfaces products a favorite of building owners who had been searching for alternatives to VCT and carpeting. The fact that it happens to boast recycled content that is among the highest in the flooring business was a benefit that didn't catch on until the green building movement recently gained traction.

ECOsurfaces flooring is comprised of post-consumer tire rubber and ColorMill® EPDM, made from post industrial waste and organic fillers. These materials are bound together using a water based polyurethane polymer. The product line is produced using a low embodied energy manufacturing process that uses minimal water, avoids heat and reuses in-line scrap to decrease waste. The result is beautiful, environmentally responsible commercial flooring that passes the strictest tests for indoor air quality, low-VOC emissions and is recyclable.

Custom colors and logos are easily achieved with ECOsurfaces Commercial Flooring. And for the ultimate in versatility, the new ECOshapes collection gives designers the ability to achieve the look of a custom floor with a fraction of the effort. These pre-cut shapes, in a variety of color patterns, provide quick and easy out-of-the-box options, for stunning floor creations.

Ecore International
715 Fountain Avenue
PO Box 989
Lancaster, PA 17601
USA

www.ecosurfaces.com
Tel: +1 717-295-3400
Fax: +1 717-295-3414

Microsorber® is a system of transparent, translucent and printed foils and acrylic glass panels which reduce reflected sound and reverberation time in buildings. It is easy to install and versatile. It allows visions of transparency and open space to come true while meeting demands of acoustics.

The high-performance sound insulation effected by Microsorber® results from its micro-perforation. The foil and acrylic glass elements have holes measuring anywhere between 0.2 mm and 0.8 mm in diameter. As soon as sound waves strike the Microsorber®, a physical reaction takes place; the sound energy is converted into heat through the friction arising at the hole edges. Reverberation times and sound levels are reduced significantly.

Whether in open-plan offices, canteens, swimming pools, production sites or entrance halls – the Microsorber® principle of transparent sound absorption allows for creativity in the design of buildings where room acoustics play a crucial role. It is also ideal as a means of optimizing the room acoustics of already existing buildings.

Microsorber® can be installed in front of walls and glass façades and below ceilings. Various systems for fastening the foil make it possible to attach and detach individual elements with ease.

1. NRW Bank, Düsseldorf, Architects: RKW Rhode Kellermann Wasrowsky Architektur + Städtebau
2. Roofing of the Schlüterhof courtyard in the Zeughaus, Berlin, German Historical Museum. Architect: I.M. Pei, New York
3. Nord/LB offices, Hannover, Architects: Behnisch, Behnisch und Partner, Stuttgart

Kaefer Construction GmbH
Dep. Microsorber
Am Lunedeich 151b
27572 Bremerhaven
Germany

www.microsorber.com
Tel: +49 (0) 471-799-5601
Fax +49 (0) 471-799-5604
E-mail: info@microsorber.com

hanabi

Nendo

Lighting from shape-memory alloy

The heat of the bulb makes this shape-memory alloy lamp "bloom" whenever the light is turned on. "hanabi", the Japanese word for "fireworks", literally means "flower + fire." Both flowers and fire fade away quickly and easily. Like its namesake, this light flickers between beauty and disappearance.

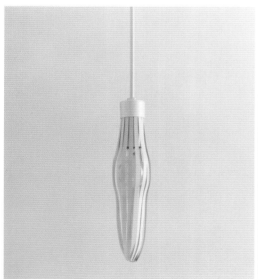

Nendo
2-2-16-5F Shimomeguro Meguro-ku
Tokyo 153-0064
Japan

www.nendo.jp
Tel: +81 (0) 36-661-3750
Fax: +81 (0) 36-661-3751
E-mail: info@nendo.jp

DuPont™ Corian® is a solid, non-porous, homogeneous surfacing material composed of ± 1/3 acrylic resin (also known as PolyMethyl MethAcrylate or PMMA) and ± 2/3 natural minerals. The main mineral is Aluminum TriHydrate(ATH) derived from bauxite, an ore from which aluminum is produced.

DuPont™ Corian® cannot delaminate and stands up well to daily wear and tear. It resists most of the impacts, nicks and cuts that occur in heavy traffic areas. DuPont™ Corian® is a non-porous material. It is solid through its entire thickness and can be fabricated with inconspicuous seams, rendering its surface hygienic. DuPont™ Corian® surfaces do not support the growth of bacteria or fungi.

DuPont™ Corian® is an inert and nontoxic material. Under normal temperature conditions, it does not emit gases. When burned, it releases mainly carbon oxides and the smoke generated is optically light and does not contain toxic halogenated gases. Because of these properties, DuPont™ Corian® is used in public areas and for sensitive applications such as airport check-in counters, walls and work surfaces in hospitals and hotels.

Colors and patterns run through the entire thickness of the material and cannot wear away. Pieces of DuPont™ Corian® can be glued together inconspicuously to create a seamless look, giving virtually unlimited design possibilities for surfaces. DuPont™ Corian® can be thermoformed in wooden or metal molds at controlled temperatures in order to create various 2D and 3D design objects. Embossing effects can also be created using the Bas Relief technique.

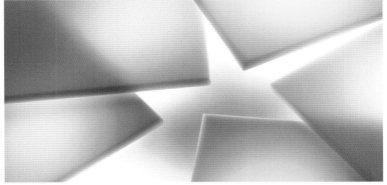

www.corian.com

HI-MACS® Natural Acrylic Stone™ is a stain-resistant, finished solid surface, ideal for countertops, vanities, and many other applications subject to the hazards of moisture and heavy wear.

HI-MACS is designed for use in residential and commercial applications and is now the horizontal and vertical surface material of choice for installers, fabricators, architects, designers and specifiers. HI-MACS is engineered to meet the demands of a multitude of commercial and residential applications. It performs well in drop ball impact tests, resists most chemical exposure, has a high UV resistance and color fastness and is resistant to water, dirt and moisture.

HI-MACS Natural Acrylic Stone is a non-toxic material and has no surface-acting agents - even over prolonged exposure. Its non-porous surface and seamless joins offer optimum hygiene. It is also available in specially treated antibacterial grades for specialized installations.

Preheating turns HI-MACS into a material that can be bent into virtually any shape and cooled without any loss of performance. HI-MACS maintains the same consistency throughout the thickness of the material. Inconspicuous seams ensure that even complex installations appear as a solid whole. The translucent properties of HI-MACS open up new possibilities for designers and architects.

2

1

3

www.lghimacs.eu

1. Oxygen Night Club. Designed and fabricated by Edge Projects Ltd.
2. A bedroom made entirely of LG HI-MACS® presented at the Hogatec international hotel, gastronomy and catering trade fair in 2008 by JOI-Design.
3. Wates Interiors Ltd. London offices.
4. Porsche-Museum. Architect Delugan Meissl
5. Hôtel Nevaï, Verbier, Switzerland. Renovation by Yasmine Mahmoudieh.

HeatSeat, WarmUpTables

J. MAYER H.

Furniture with thermochromic paint

These two projects by the german architects J. MAYER H. are a great example of the creative use of thermochromic paint, a smart material once used for thermometers and sunglasses. Thermochromic materials change thjeir color when they absorb heat. As in all smart materials the change is reversible and does not fatigue the material.

Warm-Up-Tables
Armory Art Fair, Henry Urbach Gallery, New York, USA, 2002
Courtesy Galerie Magnus Müller, Berlin

HeatSeat
Temperature Sensitive Object
Archilab, Orléans, France, 2001
Project team: Jürgen Mayer H., Marcus Bonauer, Hans Weibel
Permanent collection of San Francisco Museum of Modern Art, San Francisco, USA
Courtesy Galerie Magnus Müller, Berlin

1

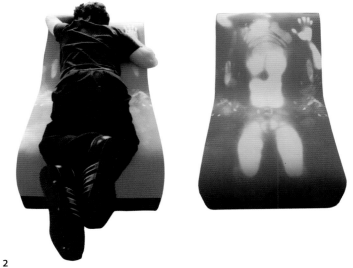

2

1. The surface of the WarmUpTable.
2. HeatSeat.
3. WarmUpTables.

3

J. MAYER H.
Bleibtreustrasse 54
10623 Berlin
Germany

www.jmayerh.de
Tel: +49 (0)30-644-9077-00
Fax: +49 (0)30-644-9077-11
E-mail: contact@jmayerh.de

Zeoform is made from 100% cellulose (derived from plants, hemp, paper, rags or other recycled sources) and water – with no glues, binders, chemicals, additives or synthetics. The molecules of Zeoform are bonded together using nano-technology capable of being made into a wide range of structural and aesthetic forms; from thin, flexible, transluscent grades for elegant lighting sytems to ebony-hard, multi-colored applicaitons for jewellery, musical instruments, speakers, furniture, homewares, automotive parts, building materials...even new computers or mobile phone casing.

The product not only creates no waste – every particle, even the dust from finishing can be recycled into a fresh new product – but each item made actually locks in carbon atoms, thus reducing emmissions and contributing to a cooler earth. Manual, semi or fully-automated ZEO-factories can be set up in any country or region, from a remote African villiage to the most industrialised precinct, to supply retail outlets or customers directly seeking beautiful, high-quality and durable products at an affordable price.

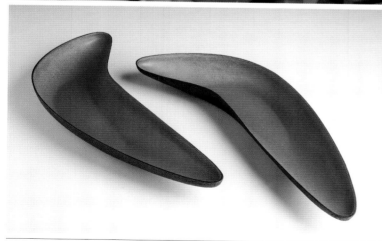

Zeo International
PO Box 1069
Mullumbimby
NSW 2482
Australia

www.zeo-international.com
Tel: +61 26-684-4553

Texture Bank

Fabrice Covelli

3-dimensional, non-computer generated textures for different materials

The Texture Bank is a line of more than 50 original 3-dimensional, non-computer generated textures designed by Fabrice Covelli that can be applied to different materials for various industrial and manufacturing processes. This collection demonstrates a wide range of design capabilities with organic or abstract references. Variations of existing designs and client specifications may be developed for differing products, materials, sizes and texture thicknesses. All of the designs can be easily applied to both translucent and opaque materials. Designs can be applied through a variety of different processes, including embossing or digital manufacturing.

Chopped Cans is made of recycled aluminum cans mixed with acrylic resin to create a 1" thick material that would be an ideal table or counter top in the hospitality industry. Different degrees of transparency can be achieved by changing the density of shredded material inside the panel for vertical applications.

Web-Cloth: Web-cloth is made of modified fabric to create a distinct web-like pattern that is then embedded into resin. Panels can be cut at any size and reassembled for a seamless and tillable design.

MiniMess is composed of thousands of letters, numbers and symbols (1/4" tall) that are randomly juxtaposed to create a playful and intriguing texture. Initially designed for placemats and coasters, the MiniMess design has also been applied to lampshades.

Branches, Broken Shells, Pine Ends, Bamboo/Reeds: In the Organic texture series, natural materials are slightly manipulated and artistically reorganized within various specifications of density and thickness. These representational designs are ideal decorative textures for environments or products with natural themes.

Rings, Crust, Circles, Shield: In the Abstract series, notions like movement, playfulness, and randomness are used to create textures with depth, intensity, and strong imaginary content. These abstract designs are warm and inviting textures that can be applied to any surface.

1

1. Bamboo reeds.
2. Pine Ends.
3. MiniMess.
4. Crust.
5. Branches.
6. Chopped Cans.
7. Web Cloth.
8. Circles.
9. Rings.

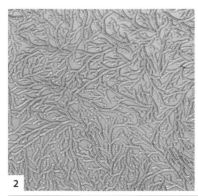

2

3

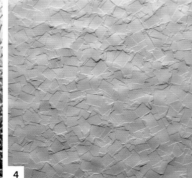

4

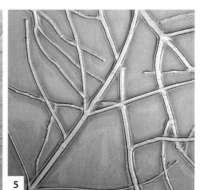

5

Fproduct, Inc - Fabrice Covelli
250 Saint Marks Avenue
Brooklyn NY 11238
USA

www.fproduct.net
Tel: +1 917-202-2349
E-mail: getinfo@fproduct.net

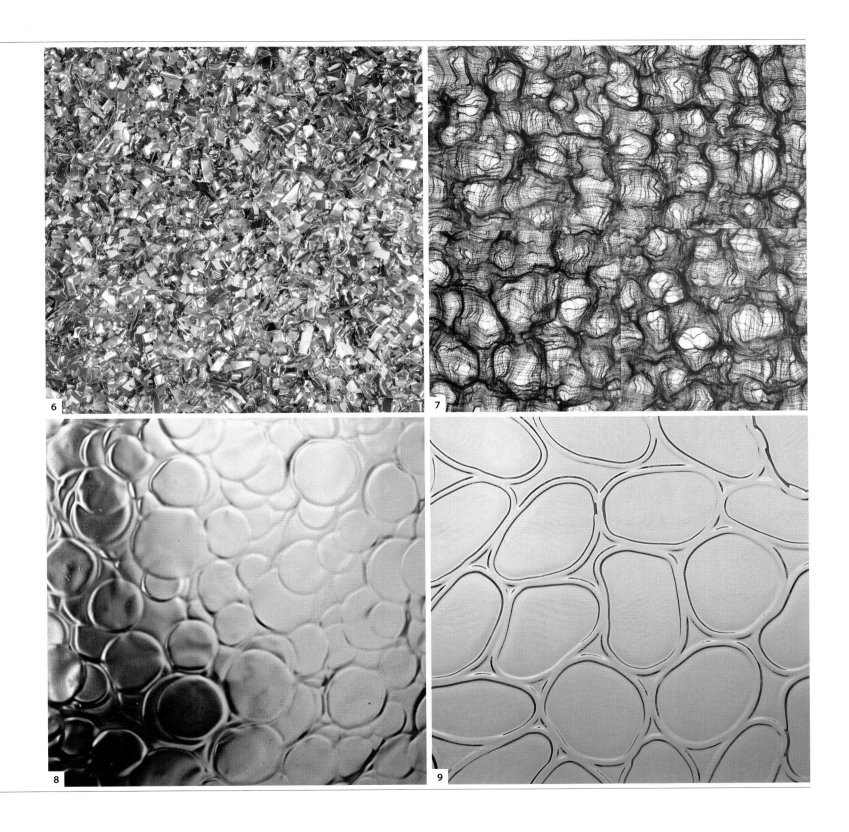

Textiles have always been present in architectural spaces and are a defining element of most interiors. However, they are often overlooked by architects who tend to focus on the "hard" parts of buildings. Recently, this has started to change with the appearance of technical textiles and a great variety of designs, materials and textures.

The term textile does not refer so much to the base material as to the method of its production (weaving and knitting). Textile fibers usually come from animals. Plant fibers (cellulose-based) have also been used since time immemorial and are still in use. Today, other kinds of fiber, metal, vinyl, nylon, rubber, etc. are also being used. Woven textiles consist of two groups of parallel threads running perpendicular to each other. The pattern in which the threads are woven is called the weave type and is important in determining the characteristics of the textile.

Knitted textiles are made of threads that run in one direction and are linked by curvilinear loops. The two common types of knitting are weft-knit and warp-knit.

Non-woven textiles are quite common in architectural applications. These textiles are produced by matting fibers with pressure, heat or gluing. Felt is the most common non-woven textile but many others are available and the field is constantly being developed and innovated. Waterproofing, self-cleaning and extra strength are properties sought in both construction and clothing. Many textiles are also being created with different fiber materials. Fiber optics and LEDs are used to create luminous textiles. Recycled materials such as tires can be used as threads. Experiments in smart textiles (thermochromic, shape memory, energy-harvesting) that started in the clothing industry are also finding their place in architecture.

Plain weave

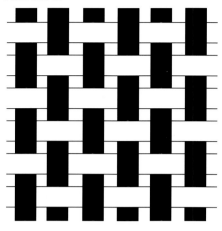

Twill weave

Satin weave

Welt-knitted

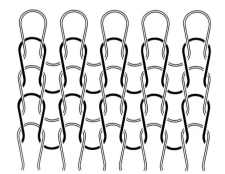

Warp-knitted

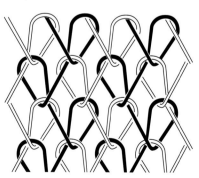

North Tiles from Kvadrat are a new way of creating and dividing space. North Tiles are a system of foam and fabric building blocks which can be put together and used as walls, decoration or for dividing rooms. North Tiles also have an acoustic function, as the fabric has a sound-absorbing effect. Each North Tile consists of a foam core laminated with fabric. The system consists of four products: a main tile, a top/bottom tile, a side tile and a corner tile.

North Tiles were designed by French brothers, Ronan and Erwan Bouroullec, and were originally created for Kvadrat's new showroom in Stockholm which opened in February 2006. The two designers were given creative freedom and the result was an impressive showroom that demonstrated a new and unique way of using fabric.

North Tiles create a dramatic and tactile look, transforming the space they are used in. The pieces are assembled with the help of a simple and flexible folding system which means that the design of the fabric surfaces is limited only by one's imagination. The fabric surfaces can be taken apart and put back together, giving the product a high level of variability.

North Tiles were accepted into The Museum of Modern Art's design collection in New York. In addition to Kvadrat's showroom in Stockholm, North Tiles were used to construct an indoor pavilion at Musée d'Art Moderne in Luxembourg in 2006, as well as for a project at the Pompidou Centre in Paris in 2007.

Kvadrat A/S
Lundbergsvej 10
DK-8400
Ebeltoft
Denmark

www.kvadrat.dk
Tel: +45 89-531-866
Fax: +45 89-531-800
E-mail: kvadrat@kvadrat.dk

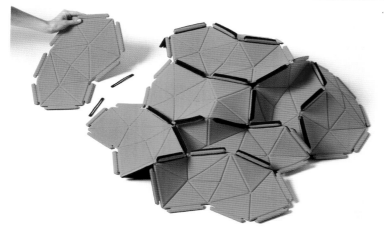

In collaboration with Kvadrat, internationally acclaimed designers Ronan and Erwan Bouroullec have created Clouds, an innovative, interlocking fabric tile concept for the home. Clouds can be used as an installation and be hung from a wall or ceiling.

The tiles are made of one element and are attached by special rubber bands. Customers can creating their own pieces quickly and easily, whether for a simple design or a complex decorative screen or wall. The tiles can be easily arranged and re-arranged to reflect individual styles and bring new ideas to the home.

Clouds was conceived when the French brothers were working with Kvadrat on the North Tiles project and were inspired to create a lighter version for the home market.

"Once in a while I flip through a design or architecture magazine, and I am often scared by all of the cold rooms," says Ronan Bouroullec. "Therefore, when we got the Kvadrat assignment we wanted to create a design solution that is both soft and welcoming. At the same time, we aimed to design a solution that was so simple and well thought out that it didn't require expensive workmen, but could be set up by everyday people without having to be polished, adjusted or given additional treatment."

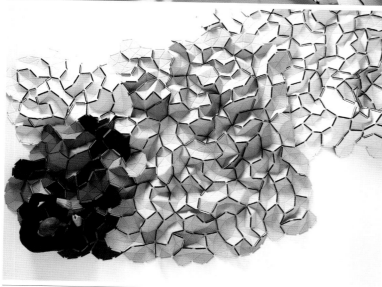

Kvadrat A/S
Lundbergsvej 10
DK-8400
Ebeltoft
Denmark

www.kvadrat.dk
Tel: +45 89-531-866
Fax: +45 89-531-800
E-mail: kvadrat@kvadrat.dk

drapilux air

Drapilux

Air-cleaning textile

The air-cleansing fabric drapilux air eliminates hazardous chemical from the air in the room. Research shows that contaminants like formaldehyde, acetaldehyde and nicotine cause unconscious escape reflexes not only in animals but also in humans. Thanks to metallic salts and oxides incorporated in the fibre, unpleasantly odoros and noxious substances such as formaldehyde or ammonia are transformed into non-toxic substances.

drapilux GmbH
Hansestraße 87
48282 Emsdetten
Germany

www.drapilux.com
Tel: +49 (0)257-292-70
Fax: +49 (0)257-292-7445
E-mail: export@drapilux.com

Drapilux bioaktiv combines optics and functions. The antibacterial decorative fabrics are suitable especially for use in hospitals and care facilities.

The textiles in contact with the skin are completely safe. There are no reactions, on the contrary - the fabrics even reduce the risk of allergies. Built-in silver ions in the Trevira-fiber decimate bacteria on the fabric surface. This fabric has been checked and certified by the TÜV Rhineland (Technical Control Board). The textiles can be washed at 60 degrees without losing their effectiveness.

drapilux GmbH
Hansestraße 87
48282 Emsdetten
Germany

www.drapilux.com
Tel: +49 (0)257-292-70
Fax: +49 (0)257-292-7445
E-mail: export@drapilux.com

NanoSphere®

Schoeller Technologies

Protective textile finish

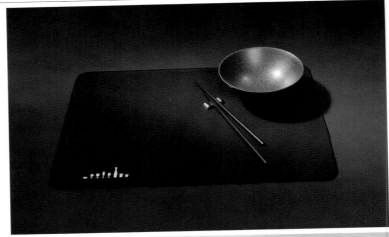

The leaves of certain plants always stay clean, because dirt cannot adhere to their finely structured surfaces and is easily washed off by rain. This natural non-stick and cleaning process, also known as the self-cleaning effect, is permanently transferred to the textile surface by means of nanotechnology.

The result is called NanoSphere®. Public areas come in for high levels of traffic and are subject to particularly intensive wear and tear. The textiles used in these areas therefore need additional protection – functionality as offered by NanoSphere®. Because, due to a specially-tuned formula, the NanoSphere® finish generates a self-cleaning effect and is also characterized by extremely good abrasion proofing. Textiles of this kind repel water and stains, stay clean for longer, need less care and have a longer service life.

1. The classic surface: The contact surface of a water drop or a particle of dirt with the textile, and therefore the level of adhesion, is very large. As a result, water or dirt adheres to the textile.
2. The NanoSphere® surface: Water drops or particles of dirt lie only on the peaks of the nano particles, and therefore have a lower contact area. Adhesion is significantly reduced, water runs off, dirt is repelled or can simply be rinsed off.

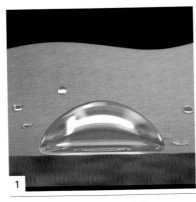

1

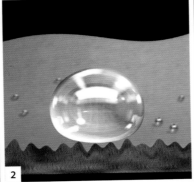

2

Schoeller Technologies AG
Bahnhofstrasse 17
CH-9475 Sevelen
Switzerland

www.nano-sphere.ch
Tel: +41 (0)81-786-0950
Fax: +41 (0)81-786-0951
E-mail: info@nano-sphere.ch

1

2

3

The lotus plant's extraordinary ability to keep itself clean by means of the ultrafine surface structures on its leaves has led to Buddhism's holy flower becoming a reference for material design. Learning from nature's example, science has recognized that it is not the smoothest possible surfaces but those with structures measuring some dozens of nanometers that repel dirt and water most effectively.

About ten years ago, dirt repellent wall paints were the first marketed products to technically utilize this self-cleaning effect. With Mincor® TX TT, BASF is now starting a new chapter: this innovative finishing material endows technical textiles for awnings, sunshades, sails and tents with the same self-cleaning effect as the lotus. What on the surface of the plant leaves are tiny papillae, on treated textiles are innumerable particles with a diameter of less than 100 nanometers embedded in a carrier matrix. Whether nature or technology – the effect is the same: these tiny nubs keep water droplets and particles of dirt at bay.

In 2006, polyester awning fabrics finished with Mincor® TX TT were very successful in achieving the transition from the laboratory to practical application, and fabrics for sunshades and sails treated with Mincor® TX TT are also now in the trial phase.

1. At first sight, polyester fabric finished with Mincor® TX TT looks unchanged (electron micrograph 500 µm).

2. More than 80% of the textile is covered with a nanoporous layer (electron micrograph, 0.5 µm = 500 nm).

3. Water droplets on a polyester fabric finished with Mincor® TX TT.

4. Self-cleaning effect: a water droplet on the leaf of the taro plant (Asiatic tuber plant).

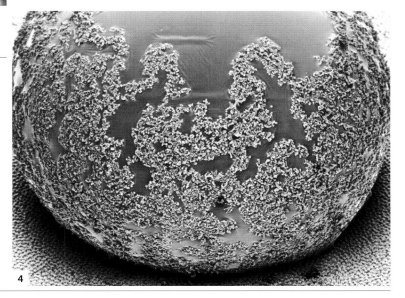

4

www.basf.com

Tel: +49 (0)621-600

Fax: +49 (0)621-604-2525

Architextile

Aleksandra Gaca

Three dimensional acoustic textile

Architextile is the latest collection of three dimensional weave structures by textile designer Aleksandra Gaca. Her research into the technical possibilities and applications of dimensional textile resulted this time in surprising combinations of contrasts. High tech in combination with natural materials, technical next to more traditional solutions, and a cool, detached character versus warm and inviting.

The Architextile collection consists of a number of fixed patterns: Tero, Šelo, Floro, Ondo and Ovalo. Most fabrics are two-sided and perfectly applicable as exclusive, autonomous interior objects, like a dividing wall or screen.

The collection also has acoustic qualities. Those, in combination with a robust firmness, make these fabrics particularly qualified to be used as wall screens or wall coverings in an architectural environment.

Aleksandra Gaca has always been fascinated by three dimensional weave structures and through the years this fascination has become more and more prominent in her work. She experiments with weaves she develops herself as well as with unusual materials. She combines technical qualities with a highly developed touch for material, dimension and beauty. Her inspiration she draws from abstract architectural concepts such as structure and repetition as well as from more dynamic concepts as dance, drama and movement.

1

1. Ovalo - acoustic wall decoration, private house, Amsterdam 2007, © Jeltje Fotografie.
2. Tero - acoustic wall decoration, INBO architects office, Las Palmas, Rotterdam 2007, © Stijn Kriele.
3. Ondo. © Aleksandra Gaca.
4. Šelo. © Aleksandra Gaca.
5. Floro. © Aleksandra Gaca.
6. Tero. © Aleksandra Gaca.

2

Aleksandra Gaca
Hooikade 13 – 1.05
2627 AB Delft
The Netherlands

www.aleksandragaca.nl
Tel/ Fax: +31 (0)15-251-1502
E-mail: a.gaca@planet.nl

The Bicicleta collection was born out of research into the possibility of using recycled rubber to create new textures. nanimarquina has made a commitment to the development of sustainable design with the carpet design Bicicleta, woven with recycled bicycle inner tubes. Producing this model, designed by Nani Marquina and Ariadna Miquel, requires between 130 and 140 bicycle inner tubes which, once collected, are washed, cut and worked on a loom.

The idea for the design came during a trip to India where the bicycle is the most common mode of transport. The production of the carpet is contributing to putting an end to waste rubber in the form of inner tubes from the city of Panipat, in the north of India, where this model is produced.

This exclusive design makes it possible to transfer rubber from the garbage in the village streets to the living rooms, studios and terraces of houses across half the world.

nanimarquina
Esglesia 10, 3er D
08024 Barcelona
Spain

www.nanimarquina.com
Tel: +34 932-376-465
Fax: +34 932-175-774
E-mail: info@nanimarquina.com

Atex is made from a combination of glass-based fabric and a silicone coating where the main ingredients are silicon dioxide, aluminum oxide and calcium oxide which are three of the most naturally abundant resources available, these are found in clay, quartz and sand, PD Interglas believes that this and the fact that Atex is fully recyclable without the need of further additives makes Atex one of the most sustainable and environmentally friendly products in the architectural textile market.

Silicone coated glass fabrics are highly flexible, do not leave any marks when folded and offer good translucency. They are non toxic and even at high temperature or during combustion they do not emit any toxic gases. Glass fabrics are inherently non-combustible. To achieve the maximum fire retardancy with the silicone rubber additional fire retardants are incorporated.

There are 5 standard grades of Atex which differ in weight, strength, translucency and openness. All the grades can be supplied with a specific coating (such as AERO to make the fabric completely airtight or as DTC – dry top coat) or color.

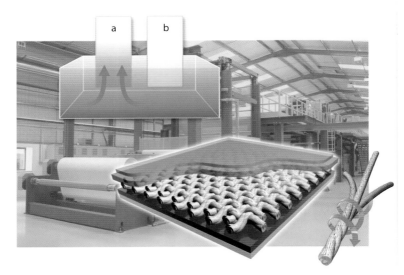

a. In standard silicone-coated glass fabric liquid rises by capilary action.
b. In Atex TRL fabric with wick resistance treatment there is no capilary rise from either warp or weft direction.

1. Bus shelter in Blackpool, UK.
2. Zenith Europe in Strasbourg, France. This multi-purpose arena is France's largest tensioned-fabric structure and it is literally designed to shine. It used 15 000 sqm of orange fabric which was fabricated around the concrete core building making the arena not just a simple venue but an eye-catching landmark. The project required a fabric that not only offered translucency (to create spectacular light effects in the dark) but that would be durable, non combustible, maintainable, affordable, with a long lifespan. The fabric chosen for that project was Atex® 5000.
3. Alexandra Palace, London/England – Atex Screen white
4. Covered car parking for rail station, Montreux, Switzerland, Luscher Architectes SA. Use of Atex 5000 Aero fibreglass membrane.

P-D Interglas Technologies Ltd
Sherborne
Dorset
DT9 3RB
UK

www.atex-membranes.com
Tel: +44 (0)193-581-1896
Fax: +44 (0)193-581-1822

2

3

4

Soft House

Kennedy & Violich Architecture

Energy-harvesting and light-emitting textile

The Soft House by KVA MATx transforms the household curtain into a set of energy-harvesting and light-emitting textiles that power solid state lighting and portable work tools such as laptops, digital cameras, and PDAs. Soft House textiles can adapt to the changing space needs of home owners and can be moved to follow the sun generating up to 16 000 watt-hours of electricity – more than half of the daily power needs of an average household.

KVA MATx application designs for energy-efficient semi-conductor technologies in movable curtains, translucent textile screens and luminous room enclosures shift the boundaries between the traditional wall and household utilities. The Soft House distributed energy network is made of multiple, adaptable and co-operative light emitting textiles that can be touched, moved and used by home owners according to their needs. Translucent movable curtains along the Soft House perimeter convert sun light into energy throughout the day, shading the house in summer and creating an insulating air layer in winter. A central curtain moves vertically to create an energy harvesting chamber or a suspended soft chandelier with integral solid state lighting.

The principles of the Soft House energy network – simplicity, adaptability, and intelligent co-operation among individual elements – are extended into the architectural design and fabrication of the Soft House. Parametric design software, developed for the Soft House project, allows the OPV density of the energy harvesting textiles to be mass customized on computerized lamination machines according to the home owner's budget and energy needs.

1. Full-Scale Energy Harvesting Textile Prototype charging during daytime.
2. Mobile energy harvesting curtains illuminate the Soft House.
3. Full-Scale Energy Harvesting Textile Prototype.
4. Detail of the full-scale prototype.

Kennedy & Violich Architecture Ltd.
10 Farnham Street
Boston MA 02119
USA

www.kvarch.net
Tel: +1 617-442-0800
Fax: +1 617-442-0808
E-mail: info@ kvarch.net

Experimental Sound Surface

Hodgetts and Fung Design and Architecture

Wool felt soud-absorbing surface

The objective of the project was to improve the acoustic qual-ity of SCI-Arc's (Southern California Institute of Architecture) Main Space and increase flexibility for amplified sound as well as normal speech. The solution needed to address the various activities that take place there, including lectures, performances, presentations, and every day conversation.

The architects designed a wool-felt partition that is suspended mid-air and constructed of various panels to prevent the ricochet effect of sound. Supported by a lightweight aluminum truss sys-tem, the wool felt is 2 cm (0.75 in) thick and features a multitude of openings on its surface to create air pockets and provide sound absorbency. The material was prefabricated off-site and later in-stalled with the help of SCI-Arc architecture students and SCI-Arc faculty member Alexis Rochas, and with the financial assistance of the Keck Foundation.

Once installed, the material was manipulated and configured into a dynamic curvy surface to further help the diffusion of sound. The fabric, which is relatively fragile, depended on the novel use of a "fastening device", typically used in industrial applications. The fastening device redistributed weight loads into the felt material while also securing it into the bending spines of the substructure.

www.hplusf.com

Annemette Beck studio produces unusual and one-of-a-kind upholstery fabrics, rugs, curtains, blankets and room dividers. The fabrics are a combination of natural materials such as paper yarn, wool, felted wool, silk, cotton and copper together with peculiar materials such as plant fibers, rubber and bicycle tubes. Annemette Beck studio works from the basic principles of weaving and experiment with new combinations of structures and materials.

Annemette Beck
Lindehuswej 5
5750 Ringe
Denmark

www.annemette-beck.dk
Tel: +45 62-641-564
Fax: +45 62-641-562
E-mail: info@annemette-beck.dk

LifeLine

Upofloor

Heavy duty PVC-free floors

LifeLine™ tile is made for heavy duty commercial floors. It is the first collection made of a new flooring material, Enomer™, which consists of 80% natural minerals and 20% PVC-free thermoplastic polymers. LifeLine is ideal for heavy wear public premises, such as department stores, schools, offices, hospitals, day care centres, etc. Enomer is a heterogeneous flooring material with a compact, ionomer impregnated wear layer. The product structure gives Life-Line flooring superior wear, scratch and maintenance properties along with an excellent dimensional stability and easy installation. Because of its low flame spread and low smoke and heat production, LifeLine has attained high fire ratings, and it complies with the IMO regulations for use in ships. LineLine's resistance to fire outperforms traditional vinyl, linoleum and rubber floorings.

Throughout its life cycle, LifeLine flooring material is ecologically safe. Because it is primarily composed of natural minerals, it is recyclable during production, can be disposed of by burning, and can be used as energy producing waste. It contains no PVC, halogens, chlorine, plasticizers, or heavy metals, and emissions in indoor environments are minimal.

The LifeLine tile size is 500 × 500 mm and thickness 2 mm. Because of the tile form LifeLine is easy to handle, and the large tile size makes for quick installation.

The first LifeLine collection features a timeless, non-directional chip design in 20 attractive colors. The range of colors is varied and versatile, with modern bright colors as well as more subdued alternatives and several stylish shades of gray. The product line also includes a range of PVC-free welding rods and skirtings in matching colors.

Upofloor Oy
P.O.Box 8
FI-37101 Nokia
Finland

www.lifelinefloors.com
Tel: +35 820-740-9600
Fax: +35 820-740-9734

With more than 80% sound absorption in speech relevant frequency ranges and a footfall reduction of up to 32 dB, the innovative acoustic floor covering from longlife can make an important contribution towards improving room acoustics, particularly in large, open-plan working areas. Its special, fully textile structure with integrated comfort, heavy-felt secondary backing – which therefore offers above-average absorption characteristics – is available as loose-lay SL IQ carpeting and SL tiles, and offers both an efficient and economical alternative to conventional construction measures for improving acoustics. The ergonomic benefits are highly impressive. It offers excellent tread comfort, is particularly kind to the back and joints, and its elasticity offers exceptional impact absorption. It is ideal for standing work areas, as well as for tasks which require a large amount of standing and walking around.

In terms of aesthetics, longlife offers a great variety of contemporary designs. Following the relaunch of the Uni Basic Collection, the classic designs have also received a complete make-over in terms of coloring and the range has been extended with the addition of a variety of designs. At the same time, the range of color options has been streamlined and reduced. As longlife offers the option of delivering small quantities of special colors and bespoke designs specially created to suit the individual requirements of the customer, there is no need to offer an endless array of options in the standard range. Clarity and simplicity make it much easier for architects, planner and builders to reach the right decision.

1. Strato
2. Veto
3. Mix
4. Flow
5. Rato

longlife Teppichboden
P.O. Box 1264
41302, Nettetal
Germany

www.longlife-carpet.com
Tel: +49 215-391-830
Fax: +49 215-391-8310
E-mail: contact@longlife-carpet.com

Danskina is a company specialized in the design and production of high-quality carpets. Danskinas current rug collection is designed by six designers whose expertise ranges across the fields of textiles, fashion and interiors, and includes Giulio Ridolfo and Aleksandra Gaca.

The Danskina rugs are characteristic not only for their exceptional design but also for their daring use of materials such as paper and bamboo. Bamboo and Bambusa are the world's first rugs to be made entirely from bamboo yarn. Danskina spent 1½ years developing the products to ensure it meets the company's high quality standards. Ulf Moritz and Felix Diener have used the new material as their starting point for striking designs very much in keeping with danskina's creative aesthetic.

1. La Carice; tufted carpet, 50% wool 50% bamboo.
2. Salto; hand woven wool carpet designed by Liset van der Scheer
3. Bamboo; 100 % bamboo carpet designed by Ulf Moritz and Felix Diener.
4. Bambusa; tufted bamboo carpet designed by Felix Diener and Ulf Moritz.
5. Corale; tufted wool carpet. Designed by Christiane Müller.
6. Surprise; hand tufted wool carpet.
7. Dune; fusion bonded wool carpet by Ulf Moritz.

1

2

3

Danskina
Cruquiusweg 111m
1019 AG Amsterdam
The Netherlands

www.danskina.com
Tel: +31 205-996-420
Fax: +31 205-996-421
E-mail: info@danskina.nl

4

5

6

7

Freek

Freek

Outdoor carpet

Freek is a colorful outdoor carpet which can be used for several outdoor purposes. The carpets are made of polyethylene and nylon yarns and have a pile height of 30 mm.

Made from ultra-soft but extremely durable fibers that are UV- and water-resistant and easy to keep clean, Freek is a heavy duty carpet that is ideal for outdoor use.

FREEK has 2.250 grams fibers per square meter and a total weight of 3.865 grams per square meter.

C&F Design B.V.
Postbus 312
5050 AH Goirle
The Netherlands

www.freekupyourlife.com
Tel: +31(0)13-530-8008
E-mail: hello@freek.nl

Outdoor is a woven vinyl flooring specially designed for outdoor aplications. The material in the Outdoor Collection is specifically developed for outdoor applications. The lifetime expectancy is dependant on the amount of exposure to sunlight and temperature. The expected lifetime for fading and/or color change in Europe, Asia, North and South America is at least 5 years.

Bolon AB
Vist Industriomrade
Industrivägen 12
Ulricehamn
Sweden

www.bolol.com
Tel: +46 (0) 32-153-0400
Tel: +46 (0) 32-153-0450
E-mail: info@bolon.com

Spinnaker is a free standing room divider designed by Beat Karrer that offers unlimited connection possibilities. With a minimum of two elements to provide stability many different shapes can be created.

The frame is a zincked pipe construction with chromed fittings and feet in black ABS.

The fabric is available in three varieties: black transparent polyester net, white sound absorbing 3D Mesh polyester fabric or furniture fabric.

OFFECCT AB
Box 100
SE-543 21 Tibro
Sweden

www.offecct.se
Tel: +46 (0)5-044-1500
Fax: +46 (0)5-041-2524
E-mail: support@offecct.se, order@offecct.se

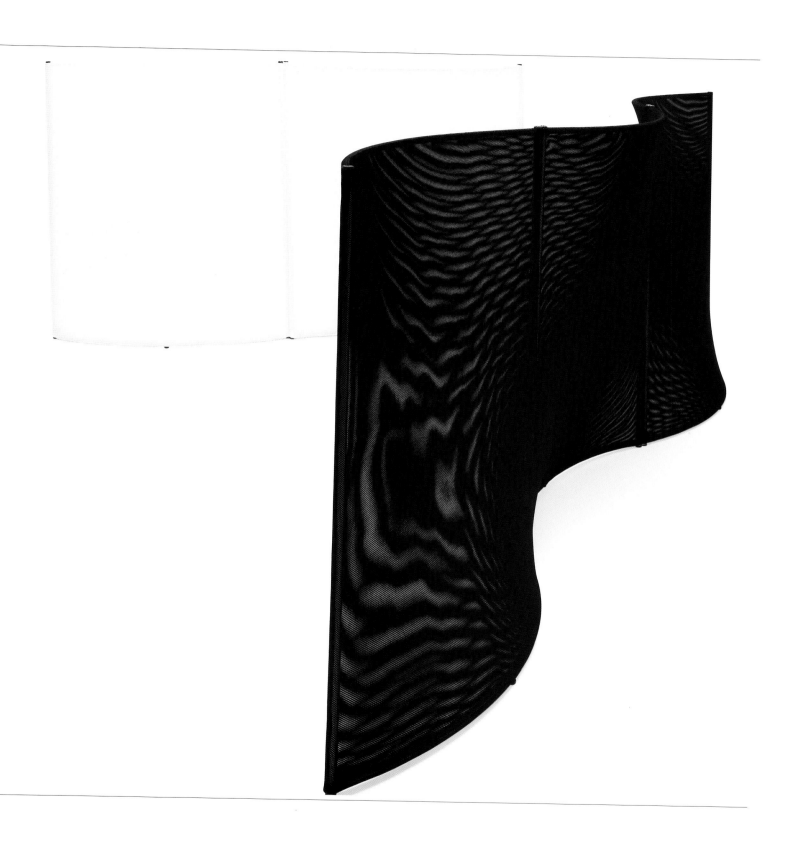

Soft Cells Broadline

Kvadrat

Wool felt soud-absorbing surface

Through its ability to absorb low frequencies, Soft Cells Broadline has a great acoustic performance. According to ISO 11654, Soft Cells Broadline is a Class-A acoustic absorber with high performance textiles.

The Kvadrat Soft Cells system is based on an aluminum frame with a concealed tensioning mechanism allowing tension to be adjusted according to fabric type, size and orientation. All frames feature a double textile layer. The quality of the textiles, combined with the cavity between the two layers, create the acoustic performance. With acoustic foam as an extra absorber behind the front textile layer, Soft Cells Broadline has improved acoustic performance, particularly for low frequencies which are often a challenge in room acoustics.

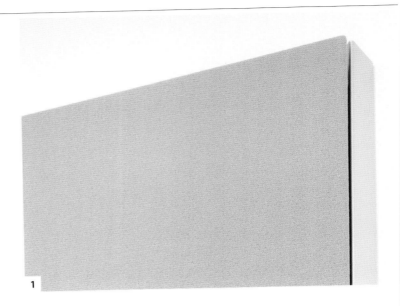

1

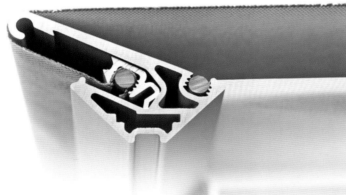

2

1. Folds and creases around corners are eliminated by a special insert which secures the excess fabric, yet the natural movement of the textile is not affected.
2. Detail of the aluminum frame.
3. Foster & Partners office, UK.
4. Concert Hall Aarhus, Denmark. C. F. Møller Architects.

3

4

Kvadrat A/S
Lundbergsvej 10
DK-8400
Ebeltoft
Denmark

www.kvadrat.dk
Tel: +45 89-531-866
Fax: +45 89-531-800
E-mail: kvadrat@kvadrat.dk

The longlife Wall Covering Collection holds grand floral and graphic patterns in attractive colors and a broad spectrum of wall coverings in solid colors. longlife's new collection is in line with a current trend: More and more textile materials are being used in commercial interiors and shop decoration. While hard and smooth surfaces have an architectural style advantage and stand for purism and clarity, textiles stand for comfort and emotional quality and determine the quality of one's stay in interiors.

Naturally the selection of materials for interiors is a matter of philosophy but it can also turn into a matter of necessity whenever good acoustics and beneficial ergonomics are required. The interplay of textile flooring systems and textile wall coverings can achieve excellent results in terms of room acoustics. The right interplay can even supersede conventional measures and otherwise necessary structural changes.

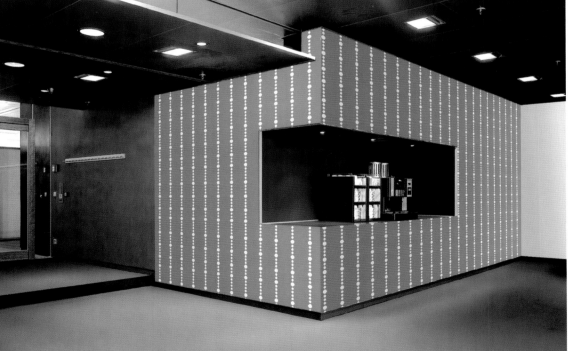

longlife Teppichboden
P.O. Box 1264
41302, Nettetal
Germany

www.longlife-carpet.com
Tel: +49 215-391-830
Fax: +49 215-391-8310
E-mail: contact@longlife-carpet.com

With people looking for more quiet and comfort in connection with modern interior design, architects and project developers of representative public buildings are now increasingly exploring possible ways of making sound absorption a feature in the design of interiors. More sound absorption means reduced dissemination of sound, and so lower noise levels.

In collaboration with the internationally recognised architect and designer, Matteo Thun of Milan, and the acoustics expert Dr Christian Nocke of the Institut für Akustik (Acoustics Institute) of Oldenburg, Ruckstuhl has been looking into possible solutions that will be in keeping both with product design requirements and with state-of-the-art spatial acoustic research. The designers were concerned not just to develop a solution to the problem in technical and acoustic terms, but also to create an attractive and functional new element as part of an ambitious interior design.

This was how the highly varied Pannello collection came into being: as an option for interior design and spatial separation, for the solution of acoustic problems and as a working resource (with the optional functions of a projection surface or pin board). Pannello gives the room a pleasant and restrained atmosphere. The size, materials and detailed design of Pannello support a wide variety of use situations for the shaping of interior spaces and the design of workstations.

When it comes to sound absorption, the properties of Pannello are outstanding: on practically the entire range of frequencies, more than 80% of the sound is absorbed. The design and the materials have been developed in such a way that both low (150 to 400 Hz) and high (400 bis 4000 Hz) tones will be absorbed in the most effective way. Made of pure virgin wool felt in subdued colors, the surface texture creates a warm and harmonious atmosphere.

1

2

3

Ruckstuhl AG
St.Urbanstrasse 21
CH-4901 Langenthal
Switzerland

www.ruckstuhl.com
Tel: +41 62-919-8600
Fax: +41 62-922-4870
E-mail: info@ruckstuhl.com

4

5

1. Capitonné: The traditional craft of upholstery gives the surface of the Pannello a structure resembling a relief.
2. Pannello Tavola.
3. Pannello sospeso: This version of Pannello, hanging freely in space, makes it possible to divide a room up into zones.
4. Wall mount.
5. Ceiling suspension
6. Pannello murale: Hung on the wall, Pannello is economical of space and at the same time highly effective, as it absorbs sound on both sides. Various accessories serve to transform Pannello into a working tool.
7. Pannello supporto: The standing version of Pannello can easily be moved from place to place.

6

7

The primary characteristic of Aeria* is its transparency to sounds. Aeria* guarantees acoustic performance of all Texaa® products by its combination of effective absorbent materials. The knit fabric used, provides flexibility and softness.

The fibers that compose this material are, by nature, flame-retardant, and produce no droplets. Texaa® products can therefore be integrated into a wide range of environments : offices, conference centers, schools, libraries, cinemas, recording studios, restaurants, etc.

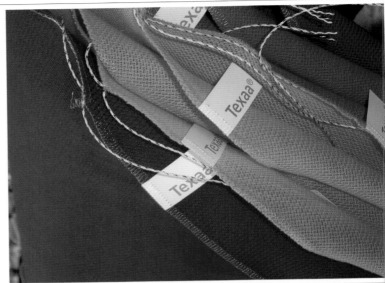

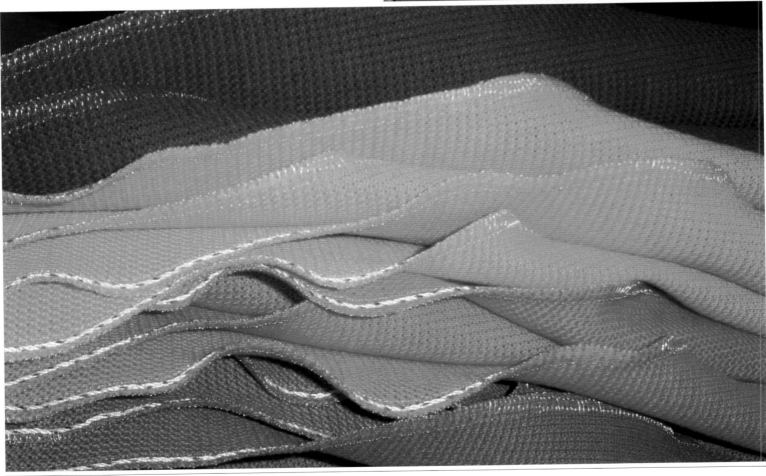

Texaa
43 Allée Mégevie
F-33174 Gradignan
France

www.texaa.com
Tel: +33 (0)55-675-7156
Fax: +33 (0)55-689-0356
E-mail: contactus@texaa.fr

The acoustic comfort of a room can normally be improved by fitting sound-absorbing materials to the surfaces (floor, walls and ceiling). However, sometimes this is not possible – either because of the layout or because of the amount of work involved – In this cases, the solution is to include objetcs within the volume.

The Stereo range of acoustic objetcs produced by Texaa® control the reverberation of sound. (Supple or rigid panels, rigid screens or room dividers, fractus tiles, totems, cubes, cones, or bricks.)

The variety of Stereo objects and the various fastening methods mean that the products can always be fitted optimally to suit the layout of a room and how it is used. Stereo products complement any environment, whether traditional or distinctly contempoary.

Texaa
43 Allée Mégevie
F-33174 Gradignan
France

www.texaa.com
Tel: +33 (0)55-675-7156
Fax: +33 (0)55-689-0356
E-mail: contactus@texaa.fr

Each panel in the Soundwave® series is designed for a specific acoustic purpose. The wall panels can be combined in different ways to meet the needs of almost any room or environment.

Flo, designed by Karim Rashid, is designed to be used as lightweight sound absorbers in the upper frequency range (500 Hz and above). These panels help reduce disturbing reflections of environmental sounds such as voices, telephones etc.

Luna, by Teppo Asikainen, is a heavyweight broadband absorber with extended efficiency in the low frequency range [150 - 500 Hz]. This panel efficiently reduces the reverberation time (sound "bouncing around") in a room.

The Mesh panel, by Teppo Asikainen, is designed to absorb lighter sounds in the higher frequencies. It is ideal for eliminating disturbing sound reflection from voices in office environments and restaurants.

Scrunch, by Teppo Asikainen, is designed to be used as a lightweight sound absorber in the upper frequency range.

Skyline, by Marre Moerel, is designed to be used as a lightweight sound absorber in the upper frequency range.

Swell, by Teppo Asikainen, is designed to be used as a lightweight sound absorber in the upper frequency range. The panel provides sound diffusion rather than absorption. Correctly positioned, the diffuser panels will improve speech intelligibility and even improve privacy in open spaces as the speaker does not need to talk loudly in order to be heard. This product is available with all components approved by the Swan eco-label.

1. Soundwave, Flo.
2. Soundwave, Luna.
3. Soundwave, Mesh.
4. Soundwave, Scrunch.
5. Soundwave, Skyline.
6. Soundwave, Swell.

1

2

OFFECCT AB
Box 100
SE-543 21 Tibro
Sweden

www.offecct.se
Tel: +46 (0)5-044-1500
Fax: +46 (0)5-041-2524
E-mail: support@offecct.se, order@offecct.se

3

4

5

6

Tensairity

Airlight

Lightweight beam element

Tensairity® is a lightweight beam element developed by Airlight Ldt. The synergetic combination of an airbeam, cables and struts leads to this lightweight structure, using very low internal pressure but with the load bearing capacity of conventional steel girders.

The central idea of Tensairity® is to use low air pressure to stabilize compression elements against buckling. The basic Tensairity® girder consists of a simple airbeam (a low pressure fabric tube), a compression element tightly connected to the airbeam and two cables running in a spiral form around the airbeam.

The protected brand name Tensairity® indicates the close relationship to the filigree structures made of struts and cables known as Tensegrity. In these structures, tension and compression are physically separated into cables and struts making the struts appear as free floating.

The simplest Tensairity® beam has a cylindrical geometry. Many other shapes are possible, too. Cigar-shaped or spindle-shaped Tensairity® beams still have a circular cross section, but are stiffer than the cylindrical structure. Tensairity® beams may well replace not just traditional steel profiles or steel girders, but also large span arch structures.

All components of the Tensairity® beam can be used to the yield limit of the material leading to exceptionally lightweight properties of this technology. Since Tensairity® beams are very simple, they have no complicated joints and no bracing elements, and are lighter than conventional girders.

Although as strong as a steel girder, Tensairity® still has many properties of a simple airbeam. Like all inflated structures Tensairity® is deployable, too. Assembling of Tensairity® beams is very easy. The beam can be designed so that no screws or rivets are needed for assembly, allowing a very fast set up. The dismantled Tensairity® beam can be compactly stored and easily transported.

Closing the loop is important. Not only the set up of Tensairity® beams is fast, the dismantling of such beams and separation of the different materials is fast and simple, too. Again, functional separation is the key. As standard procedures for the recycling of steel and aluminum exist, strong efforts are underway for an effective recycling of membranes.

1

2

1. Skiers Bridge, Lanselevillard, France. Design team: Charpente Concept SA, Barbeyer Architect.
2. Web Enclousure , Tenerife, Canary Islands, Spain. Engineering and architect: Airlight Ltd. The dome shaped structure is a deployable Tensarity; the dome is has a diameter of 11.8 m and is 6.3 m high. The structure consists of 2 identical halves: each of these is composed of 7 "banana" shaped Tenserity, inflated with an overpressure of 100 mbar when the structure is closed; the enclosure opens and closes just by inflating: no mechanical component.
3. Köngsberg Jazz Festival, Oslo, Norway. Architect: Snoetta

Airlight Ltd
Via Croce 1
CH-6710 Biasca
Switzerland

www.airlight.ch
Tel: +41 91-873-0505
Fax: +41 91-873-0509
E-mail: info@airlight.ch

3

Light

Light is of course not a proper material. It is however one of the most important elements in defining the character of any architectural space. In the form of artificial illumination, light is a technological product similar to architectural materials. Today, at the end of the era of the incandescent lamp, we are witnessing a proliferation of light sources and systems. Most new technologies are based on LED lights or the use of fiber optics. Both elements can be introduced to many materials completely changing our traditional idea of the light fixture. Today it is possible to have light-emitting textiles, luminous wall panels and luminous floors. Concrete, ceramic and plastic elements with incorporated LEDs or fiber optics are available in many designs. The control systems for lighting are, in many cases, moving away from the simple light switch. Interaction technologies and the use of sensors have found one major application and many systems with movement and temperature sensors are available. Display systems that can be incorporated as architectural elements are also becoming popular and many different technologies (holographic projections, LEDs, etc.) are in use.

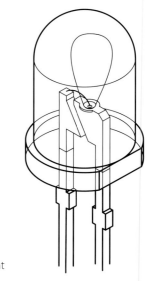

LED light

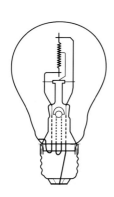

Incandescent light bulb

Halogen light bulb

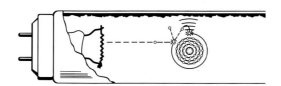

Fluorescent tube

The electromagnetic spectrum

Frequency (Hz)	Wavelength	Wave type
	0,1 Å	Gamma Rays
10^{19}		
	1 Å - 0,1 nm	
10^{18}		
	1 nm	X Rays
10^{17}		
	10 nm	
10^{16}		Ultraviolet
	100 nm	
10^{15}		Visible
	1 µm	
10^{14}		
	10 µm	Infrared
10^{13}		
	100 µm	
10^{12}		
	1 mm	
10^{11}		
	1 cm	Microwaves
10^{10}		
	10 cm	
10^{9}		
	1 m	
10^{8}		Radio, TV
	10 m	
10^{7}		
	100 m	
10^{6}		AM
	1000 m	
10^{5}		

Luminex

Luminex S.p.A.

Illuminated textile

Luminex combines technology and electronics with fabrics, using high efficient LEDs to spread light safely at very low voltages (3,6V). The supplying can be powered either with a standard power supply from the electric system, or through a commercial battery at 9V or with cells used in mobile telephone technology; small rechargeable batteries with a duration of 7-8 hours.

As often happens, the best inventions are the result of synergy and collaboration between different fields; this was the case with Luminex. The idea was to "weave the light" with optic fibers generally not used in textile manufacturing. These kinds of fibers are not stretchable, elastic and soft, all features necessary for use with looms. It has therefore been necessary to modify both the fibers and the looms in order to overcome these difficulties.

The applications of such a fabric are endless. Thanks to the spectacular aspect of the product the most obvious use is in the clothing industry, but it can also be used in staging, set designs and fairs, in hotels, and private and public furnishing, in shops, showrooms and restaurants, and even in car interiors where a suffused and spread light seems to favor better driving.

Luminex
Via dei Fossi 14/b
59100 PRATO (Po)
Italy

www.luminex.it
Tel: +39 057-473-0283
Fax: +39 057-473-0154
E-mail: info@luminex.it

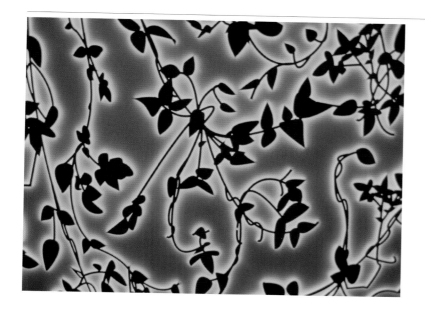

DigitalDawn is a reactive window blind with a surface that is in constant flux, growing in luminosity in response to its surroundings. It digitally emulates the process of photosynthesis using printed electroluminescent technology. The darker a space becomes the brighter the blind will glow maintaining a balance in luminosity. A natural, botanical environment appears to grow and evolve on the window lamp.

Light sensors monitor the changing light levels of the space triggering the growth of the foliage on the blind. The piece explores how changing light levels within a space can have a profound and physiological impact on our sense of well being. It also explores the ability and potential of fabric to flirt on the boundary of physical and virtual spaces as it plays with the ethereal quality of light in a continuous dialogue with its environment.

Digital Dawn was conceived to mimic the ability of plants to photosynthesise, utilizing the natural energy of the sun in the day and storing electricity that will be used later to illuminate the blind.

DigitalDawn was commissioned by Future Physical and the Royal College of Art's Innovation Unit and was presented at the Eco-Technology strand in February 2003 at Firstsite Gallery, Colchester. Since 2004 DigitalDawn has been part of the Textile collection at London's Victoria & Albert Museum.

All images: © loop.pH Ltd

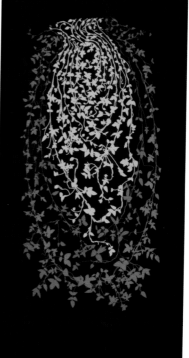

Loop.pH
Unit 2,
231 Stoke Newington Church Street
London, N16 9HP
UK

www.loop.ph
Tel: +44 207-812-9188,
E-mail: info@loop.ph

Scintilla®, Scintilla® Lumina™

Sensitile®

Acrylic polymer tile with fiber-optic elements

Hundreds of light guides are carved into a transparent block of acrylic polymer to create each Scintilla tile or panel. Ambient light and shadows are picked up by these elements and dispersed throughout the surface creating a shimmering response.

Scintilla® is available in five standard colors, which come come in standard thicknesses and are also customizable. The surface can be polished or matt. The color, size and thickness of the tiles or panels do not effect the reactivity, they provide for different effects.

Unlike standard Scintilla® products which work without electricity, Scintilla® Lumina™ combines a translucent polymer surface with a light source. Scintilla® Lumina™ redirects a single point of light into thousands illuminating the substrate with tiny, twinkling points of light.

1. Scintilla® panel.
2. Scintilla® (lumina) Bronze panel.
3. Standard lime 4 × 4 inch scintilla panel.
4. Coffee Bar Jeddah, Saudi Arabia. Designer: HRFC/ SensiTile Systems. Scintilla® Lumina™ flexible panels

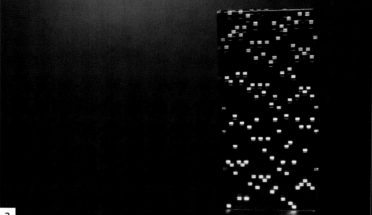

Sensitile Systems
1735 Holmes Road
Ypsilanti, MI 48198
USA

www.sensitile.com
Tel: +1 313-872-6314
Fax: +1 313-872-6315
E-mail: info@sensitile.com

1

Composed of a micro-concrete mix within which "light channels" are embedded, Terrazzo blends the durability of concrete with the latest in optical technology. Terrazzo tiles contain acrylic "light channels" embedded within concrete to transfer light from one point to another. As shadows move across Terrazzo's surface, the light channels flicker with a randomized, twinkling effect.

Terrazzo is extremely versatile and can be used almost anywhere: indoors or outdoors, on floors, walls and countertops; in short, wherever traditional tiles are used. Terrazzo comes in Tiles and Slabs. The tiles present standard sizes while the slabs are custom manufactured to specific projects. Both tiles and slabs come in standard as well as customizable colors.

Unlike standard Terrazzo products which are reactive to ambient light and shadow, achieving their effect without electricity, Terrazzo Lumina™ diffuses a single point of light into thousands. Terrazzo Lumina™ redefines the experience of concrete.

1. Terrazzo gray floor tile.
2. Terrazzo Lumina.
3. Terrazzo blue wall tile.

2

3

Sensitile Systems
1735 Holmes Road
Ypsilanti, MI 48198
USA

www.sensitile.com
Tel: +1 313-872-6314
Fax: +1 313-872-6315
E-mail: info@sensitile.com

Jali®

Sensitile®

Acrylic polymer tile with fiber-optic elements

Sensitile® products were born from the need to reconcile the relationship between ourselves and our environment. Sensitile's® materials quietly interact with ambient light and shadow creating an aesthetically pleasing solution to our utilitarian needs.

Inspired by traditional Indian perforated stone screens, the Sensitile® Jali® line of light-refractive polymer panels are a revolutionary material that bends light to create whimsical, lacelike shadows. The Sensitile® Jali® line features a repertoire of vibrant patterns, each having their own distinctive ambience. The Jali® line of acrylic tiles and panels is available in a multitude of customizable sizes and colors. Jali® patterns are also available in different densities to expand on the appearance, levels of privacy and budgets.

1. Jali® Cascata - blue emerald.
2. Jali® Mille.
3. Jali® Quadrato - clear.

Sensitile Systems
1735 Holmes Road
Ypsilanti, MI 48198
USA

www.sensitile.com
Tel: +1 313-872-6314
Fax: +1 313-872-6315
E-mail: info@sensitile.com

theANEMIX is a new lighting system that creates a three-dimensional effect inspired by bioluminescence; a combined design of light and technology. This system was developed by LUXIA, a Chilean company formed by two young architects, light designers Ximena Muñoz and Paulina Villalobos, and industrial designer Mónica Labra.

theANEMIX is an aluminium panel composed by a luminescent and a reflective layer that can be modified to create a wide range of visual effects.

The luminescent layer is screen-printed acrylic or glass, lit laterally by linear LEDs that can be colored (white, blue, green, red or yellow) or which use the RGB colour system - in other words, the same LED strip contains the three basic colours (red, green and blue) that mix with a sequencer or DMX system to obtain a very wide range of colors. The LEDs have the special feature of being an extremely small source of light for a very long duration (100,000 hours) and have very low consumption (7-14W/m).

Thermoform mirrors are placed behind this luminescent layer reflecting the serigraph's light lines, obtaining a unique effect of depth and distortion of the projected image.

theANEMIX is a modular system. It works from a 60x60cm (24X24in approximately) module that can be joined with up to six modules (1.2x1.8m or approximately 4x6ft), which allows coverage of extensive surfaces. In this manner it can cover vertical surfaces such as illuminated walls or be used as a finish on furniture. It can also cover horizontal surfaces such as false ceilings, floors or tables. It is an innovative form that gives a different image to commercial spaces such as bars, discotheques, stores, hotels and spas.

Luxia
Las Urbinas 87,
11 Providencia, Santiago
Chile

www.theanemix.com
Tel: +56 223-350-34

The range of lighting covers everything from single pixel products, to low definition products, to the "MMD range" (Multi Modular Design) and on to higher definition products. They all share the beauty of the Beadlight® diffusion system and the Ice Lighting™ visual effects engine to create single or multiple arrays of visually appealing feature lighting incorporating moving textures, flowing colors and animations. All products in the range are designed to work with one another to bring designers' unique light creations to life.

The MMD range is like a designer's palette used in the creation of unique lighting features. Currently MMD utilizes from 1 to 9 basic elements, any number of which are combined in an art form. MMD is a cost effective solution, ideal in Clubs, Casinos, Bars and Restaurants where the ambiance requires subtle mood enhancement. The MMD system is comprised of LED light sources on printed circuit boards (pcb) attached to a back board and reflecting the layout of the designer. The pcb display is powered by the Ice Lighting™ visual effects engine. Positioned in front of the pcb is the Beadlight® diffusion lens which is fixed around each aperture at the rear of the design wall.

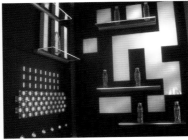

Beadlight Limited
B3-B7 New Yatt Business Centre,
Witney, Oxfordshire, OX29 6TJ
United Kingdom

www.beadlight.com
Tel: +44 (0)199-386-8866
Fax: +44 (0)199-386-8894
E-mail: contact@beadlight.com

SCHOTT's patented LightPoints™ LED glass system features light-emitting diodes (LEDs) wirelessly encapsulated inside laminated glass. Electricity flows throw a pre-structured clear conductive coating, eliminating the need for visible wiring. LED glass requires virtually no maintenance; in fact, LightPoints™ LED Glass can last decades without being replaced.

LightPoints™ LED glass is a way to add an upscale, dramatic look to locations such as airports, hotels and office buildings. The list of applications includes skylights, glass handrails, lit building façades, elevator ceilings and advertising signs.

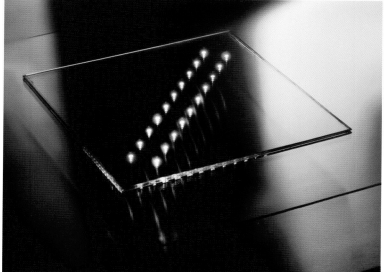

SCHOTT North America, Inc.
555 Taxter Road
Elmsford, NY 10523
USA

www.us.schott.com
Tel: +1 914-831-2200
Fax: +1 914-831-2201

SCHOTT AG
Hattenbergstrasse 10
55122 Mainz
Germany

www.schott.com
Tel: +49 (0) 613-166-0
Fax: +49 (0) 613-166-2000

Petal Pusher

ifm - Maggie Orth

Interactive textile and light installation

Petal Pusher is an interactive textile and light installation that explores the hidden electrical and transmissive properties of textiles. Each pattern is machine embroidered on DesignTex wool felt and hand tufted with electronic yarns. When viewers touch the tufted, electronic textile sensor area of each pattern, the felt and embroidered yarns are illuminated from behind, revealing the light transmissive properties of the textile. Color variation and reflection change as viewers illuminate different panels at four different light levels. Forty-nine unique patterns - all derived from a single motif - are available, in numerous configurations. Each pattern is limited to an edition of twelve.

Each patented, electronic textile sensor is made of yarn twisted with fine metal fibers that are charged with a small, harmless amount of electricity. Your body is a big bag of electrically conductive salt water. Touching the tufted sensors allows the electrical charge to flow from the yarn, through your body, to the ground. Circuitry detects this change in charge and sends an electrical signal to brighten and dim the lights.

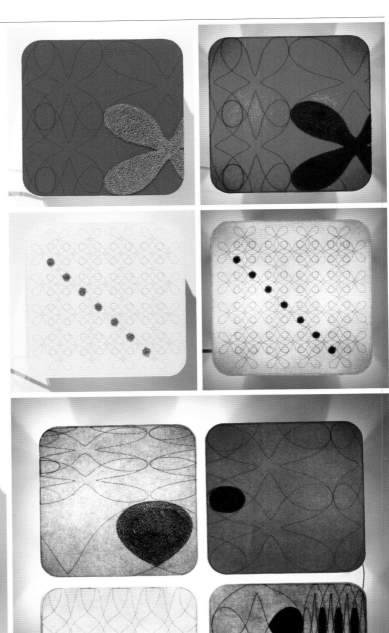

International Fashion Machines
1205 East Pike Street Suite 2G
Seattle, WA 98112
USA

www.ifmachines.com
Tel: +1 206-860-5166
E-mail: info@ifmachines.com

The patented unobtrusive frame makes this an attractive element for use in providing improved quality of artificial and natural lighting and also acoustic properties. New design preferences for using illuminated textile surfaces open up a wide range of innovative applications for architects, lighting and general interior designers.

The thinnest of joint-lines and an elliptically-shaped rigid profile are available for virtually shadow-free, uniform light distribution. The durable wrinkle-free stretched-membrane modules and 2-ply foil are dustproof and also act as sound absorbers.

Special finishing techniques and coating materials produce a high UV resistance; the product never changes color or fades. All fabrics of SEFAR® Architecture products are almost non-flammable B1 according to DIN 4102, producing nearly no smoke and no burning droplets.

Sefar AG
Hinterbissaustrasse 12
CH-9410, Heiden
Switzerland

www.sefar.com
Tel: +41 71-898-5104
Fax: +41 71-898-5871
E-mail: systems@sefararchitecture.com

A pedestrian's footprints remain visible for about a minute after crossing this interactive lightfloor by Rogier Sterk. The weight of someone walking across the floor displaces some or most of the fluid inside the top layer, leaving 'lightprints' where ever feet touch the surface. Though these prints vanish as the pedestrian proceeds, it takes about a minute for them to disappear completely.

A Lightfader floor consists of a modular system of tiles. Each one measures 1000 × 1000 × 75 mm and weighs 30 kg. The top layer is made of strong and scratch resistant material. The tiles can hold up 250 kg per square meter.

Lightfader can be applied in interior situations, in both private and public environments. Possible applications are: flooring in interior facilities, from bars, restaurants, shops and waiting rooms to cinemas and entrances to office buildings; direction indicators in department stores and airports; temporary installations like stands and catwalks.

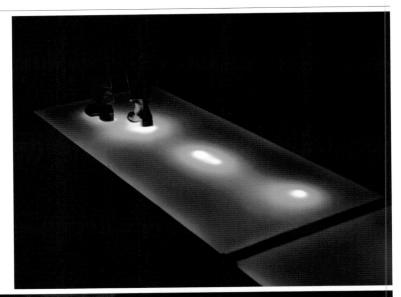

Rogier Sterk
St. Peterlaan 115
6821 HG Arnhem
The Netherlands

www.rogiersterk.nl
Tel: +31 (0)62-748-3351
E-mail: info@rogiersterk.nl

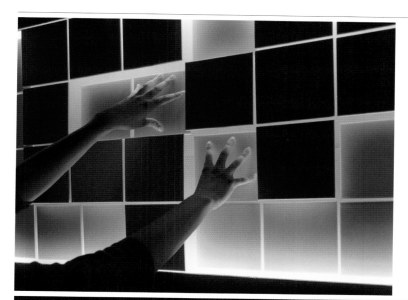

The tiles of the Tiled Wall system emit light when pressed with the hand. That way the users are able to create different patterns changing the illumination and look of the space.

Rogier Sterk
St. Peterlaan 115
6821 HG Arnhem
The Netherlands

www.rogiersterk.nl
Tel: +31 (0)62-748-3351
E-mail: info@rogiersterk.nl

The Terra LED are unglazed, ceramic tiles, manufactured according to the Ultragres-process, with integrates LED lighting. By combining this new lighting technology with Terra Maestricht tiles, floors and walls including lighting can be tiled together without having to install any fittings in advance. Grooving and cabling are not necessary. Each tile is connected to the electricity supply via a cable. LED tiles can also be laid in wet areas.

Using LED lighting has a number of benefits. A low build-in height; the thickness of the tiles and lighting enables them to be easily laid next to other tiles from the Terra Maestricht collection. They use low-tension current (24V) which means: a very low power consumption; a long life (50 000 to 100 000 burning hours); a low heat production; that they can be laid by a tile-layer; that they resist shocks and vibrations.

Lighting in floors and walls is also possible with tiles from the successful Terra Maestricht collection. LED lighting is introduced in two sizes and four colors of tiles. LED tiles allow surprising markings in tiled surfaces to be strikingly and innovatively introduced.

1-2. Terra LED tile.
3-4. Marienhospital in Osnabrück, Germany. Architect: Josef Pongratz.
5. Interior with black Terra LED tiles.

Royal Mosa
Meerssenerweg 358
6224 AL Maastricht
The Netherlands

www.mosa.nl
Tel: +31 (0) 43-368-9444
Fax: +31 (0) 43-368-9333
E-mail: servicedesk@mosa.nl

HypoSurface™

HypoSurface Corp.

Dynamic 3d display system

The C.W. Allen Group has partnered with MIT Professor and CEO of HypoSurface, Corp., Mark Goulthorpe, and his international team of designers and engineers to bring a truly innovative new marketing/sponsorship vehicle to the North American events industry.
This stunning new, multi-award winning product is called HypoSurface™ and it is a powerful visceral display medium. This is like a huge billboard where the display surface actually moves outward as much as 2 feet and can create waves that ripple across its surface at 60 mph. The HypoSurface system creates an audio, visual and physical experience that has an almost mesmerizing effect on all that witness it in action.
The physical display system of HypoSurface consists of 10 aluminium frames, each with 56 stainless steel pneumatic actuators and their manifold valves, the associated pipework and cabling, and a continuous metallic/rubber display surface, a detatchable pneumatic pipe main that distributes air to all the installed frames and the suport structure.
The HypoSurface system has been devised for ease of transport and assembly, being an essentially modular, lightweight device which is rapidly and easily fabricated by bolting the frames together and using a series of plug-and-plag pneumatic and electrical fittings.

HypoSurface Corp.
125 1/2 Spring Street
Cambridge, MA 02141
USA

www.hyposurface.org
Tel: +1-617-395-7778
E-mail: info@hyposurface.org

HoloPro™ enables projection onto glass in daylight while maintaining transparency. This is made possible by the patented HoloPro™ technology: holographic optical elements are beamed onto a highly transparent film by laser. This is then embedded in glass. The lightguiding effect enables rear projection onto the glass screen. The angle-selective effect of the HOEs means that only the projected picture is directed at the viewer. The result is a sharp, high-contrast picture – even in broad daylight.

HoloPro™ screens become a component of the light and room concept. Individual sizes and shapes create lively information areas that structure the room without disturbing its transparency and effect. The transparency of the projection surfaces will lead to creative ways of presenting information. Interactive elements with touch or gesture control extend the possible areas of use.

HoloPro™ is suitable for a multitude of different presentation applications. For example: as an information system for visitors in reception areas in combination with touch or gesture control; in room-high multimedia glass walls; as a rear-projection screen in shop windows and a screen in broad daylight.

The production of HoloPro™ in 4:3 format (up to 100") and 16:9 format (up to 128") and the manufacture to customer-specified sizes and shapes are both possible. HoloPro™ films can also be embedded in larger glass panes or special glass (e.g. hardened glass). They cannot, however, be embedded in existing glass panes. Instead, the HoloPro™ projection foil can be used in such cases.

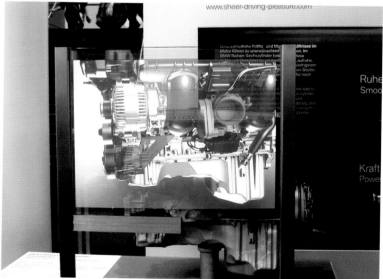

G+B pronova GmbH
Lustheide 85
51427 Bergisch Gladbach
Germany

www.holopro.com
Tel: +49 (0)220-420-4301
Fax: +49 (0)220-420-4300
E-mail: contact@gb-pronova.de

Cell Phone Disco

Informationlab

A surface that visualizes the electromagnetic field of an active mobile phone

Cell Phone Disco is a surface that visualizes the electromagnetic field of an active mobile phone. Several thousand lights illuminate when you make or receive a phone call in the vicinity of the installation.

Cell Phone Disco makes an invisible property of the environment perceptible to our senses. It reveals the communicating body of the mobile phone.

Every single mobile phone transmits radio waves in order to connect to a network and everyday millions of people around the world are broadcasting their private conversations. Although Cell Phone Disco has been embraced by art galleries and museums, its rightful place is in public space to generate a glimpse at the dynamics of this omnipresent mobile phone traffic.

Thousands of sensors that are incorporated in Cell Phone Disco are tuned to detect the mobile phone's electromagnetic radiation. Each of them sets an LED to flicker when it picks up a nearby transmission in frequency used by gsm network. Because each sensor is independent and they are applied in high density, the installation has the capacity to display the real time high-res image of the electromagnetic field. As a mirror, it reveals the actual shape of the field and enables us to witness the dynamics of each transmission.

1-2. Cell Phone Disco instalation. Photos by Max Glanville
3-4. Details of Cell Phone Disco. Photos by Informationlab

1

2

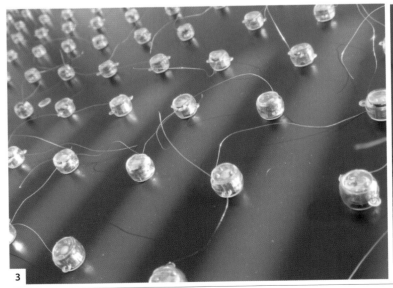

3

4

www.informationlab.org
E-mail: info@informationlab.org

The 3D Display Cube creates a true spatial display by using individually controllable light nodes in a 3D matrix.

The 3D Display Cube is a patented system that integrates LED technology to create true three-dimensional imagery and has wide spread uses with retail, signage applications, home display, and advertising. The latest version of the 3D Display Cube uses a custom LED module that allows users to snap together a spatial display of any size. This means that individual modules can be easily replaced should they go out, making the unit more architectural applicable.

A prototype is on permanent display at the Museum of Science and Innovation in Tokyo. It was also Exhibited at Chanel Mobile Art Tokyo, where it was applied to a travelling exhibition container designed by Zaha Hadid, 2008

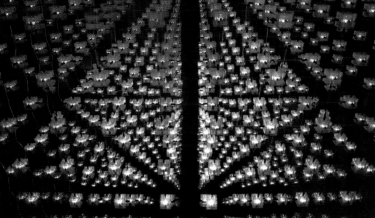

James Clar
Traffic Design Gallery
Saratoga Bldg. (behind Tamweel)
Al Barsha, UAE 6716
Dubai

www.jamesclar.com
Tel: +971 4-341-8494
Fax: +971 4-341-8566
E-mail: info@ jamesclar.com

PixelSkin 01

Orangevoid

Interactive surface and video screen

PixelSkin 01 is a heterogeneous smart surface that creates dynamic windows in response to subject states while acting simultaneously as a full color video screen. It uses a combination of Liquid Crystal (LC) glass and ultra-bright LEDs controlled by a distributed network of microcomputers and sensor consoles. As the subject approaches the surface, an onboard pyroelectric sensor turns the default translucent state of a cluster of disks to transparent. The diameter of this transparent field is dynamically adjusted according to various subjective and environmental parameters. Based on simplified biomemetic notion of swarm phenomena in nature, the control system uses what is known in the field of AI as a distributed agent-based approach where each unit in a system is assigned a limited responsive behavior, and complexity is allowed to emerge at system level. Translucent fronted glass allows uniform diffusion of the colored light emitted by the LEDs at the perimeter of each disk. Since brightness for each red, green and blue LEDs is controlled individually; each disk acts as a color pixel.

Orangevoid
66 Osbaldeston Road
London - N16 7DR
United Kingdom

www.orangevoid.org.uk
Tel: +44 (0) 207-502-2239

PixelSkin 02 is a modular surface system made of robotic pixel-tiles. Each tile consists of 4 triangular panels actuated by a 200 m Shape Memory Alloy (SMA) wire. A surface embedded micro-controller controls the opening of each pixel-tile by adjusting power-supply 20 times per second. Depending on the supplied opening-coefficient, each set of four panels acts as a pixel (255 states between fully open and fully closed). A technique called multiplexing enables each pixel-tile to be individually controlled, thus generating a surface-wide control mechanism capable of simulating low-resolution images, patterns or animations. Based on multi-layered electrographic architecture, these surfaces could create dynamic transparent fields allowing views and natural light while simultaneously generating low-resolution images, low refresh rate videos or patterns.

The work presented here explores new possibilities in media augmented surfaces with multiple function handling means and the behavior embedded into the material itself. Essentially focused on developing responsive membranes; these surfaces concentrate on inducing user enticement and participation through interaction and expressive material response. In an attempt to bridge the gap between lifeless façade automation systems and highly expressive media facades that often remain devoid of any real function, these surfaces suggest new solutions to integrate function and aesthetic expression through embedded media. Surfaces developed at Orangevoid deploy both non-mechanistic visual response, and kinetic action to merge function, information and the design expression.

Orangevoid
66 Osbaldeston Road
London - N16 7DR
United Kingdom

www.orangevoid.org.uk
Tel: +44 (0) 207-502-2239

GreenPix
Simone Giostra & Partners
Zero energy media wall

GreenPix - Zero Energy Media Wall - is a groundbreaking project applying sustainable and digital media technology to the curtain wall of the Xicui entertainment complex in Beijing, near the site of the 2008 Olympics.

The project was designed and implemented by Simone Giostra & Partners, a New York-based office with a solid reputation for its innovative curtain walls in Europe and the US, with lighting design and façade engineering by Arup in London and Beijing.

Featuring the largest color LED display worldwide and the first photovoltaic system integrated into a glass curtain wall in China, the building performs as a self-sufficient organic system, harvesting solar energy by day and using it to illuminate the screen after dark, mirroring a day's climatic cycle.

The Media Wall will provide the city of Beijing with its first venue dedicated to digital media art, while offering the most radical example of sustainable technology applied to an entire building's envelope to date.

The building will open to the public in June 2008, with a specially commissioned program of video installations and live performances by artists including: Xu Wenkai, Michael Bell Smith, Takeshi Murata, Shih Chieh Huang, Feng Mengbo and Varvara Shavrova.

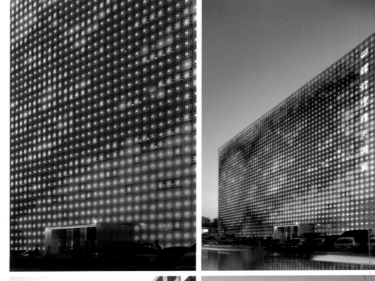

All images: © Simone Giostra & Partners and ARUP

Simone Giostra & Partners, Inc.
55 Washington Street
Suite 454
Dumbo, New York 11201
USA

www.greenpix.org
Tel/Fax: +1-212-920-8180
E-mail: info@sgp-architects.com

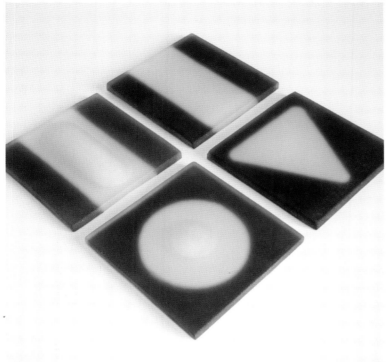

Glowway Ltd has developed a self-illuminating tile that stays luminous for several hours in the dark without any electricity. Glowway tiles have been manufactured from high quality glass or polycarbonate. By combining self-illuminating materials with glass and utilizing state of the art manufacturing technology Glowway has patented the product range for safety and orientation signs. Tests conducted by Helsinki University of Technology have shown that the tiles easily meet the international ISO 16069:2004 standard's requirements for post-illumination.

Glowway Ltd offers a set of standard designs, sizes, colors and patterns and the tiles can also be customized according to client's wishes. Glowway tiles are durable and well suited to public floor or wall use. The luminous material and different colors are integrated in the glass so that they do not wear in use when installed on floors. Thanks to the treatment of the surface the tiles are also resistant to scuffing and chemical substances. The products can be installed during construction or in constructed buildings on all kinds of concrete and stone floors. The tiles are also available with integrated pattern systems for the visually impaired.

The tiles can be used for indicating exit ways according to architecture in public buildings, airports, hospitals and underground facilities i.e. all spaces from where people need to be able to exit fast in case of emergency. The tiles can also be used for decorative purposes in homes, restaurants, nightclubs and other venues.

Glowway Oy Ltd
Pieksämäki
Finland

www.glowway.com
E-mail: info@glowway.com

Polar

Nendo

Tables with polarizing filters

This table set is named Polar because of its use of polarizing films and its icy aesthetic.

The size changes as the three side tables are stacked or lined up together. When the tables are stacked, the polarizing film inside the table top makes flower patterns appear through the clear glass surface.

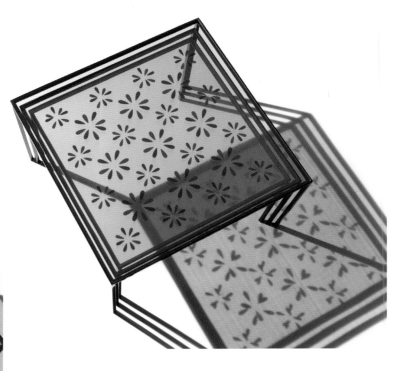

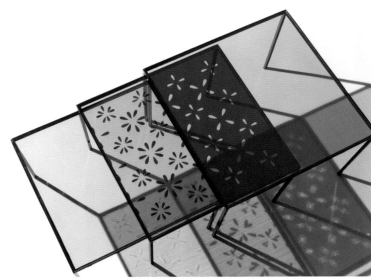

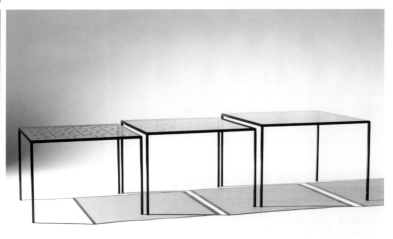

Nendo
2-2-16-5F Shimomeguro Meguro-ku
Tokyo 153-0064
Japan

www.nendo.jp
Tel: +81 (0) 36-661-3750
Fax: +81 (0) 36-661-3751
E-mail: info@nendo.jp

OR is the boldest installation at the Milan International Furniture Fair 2008, a vortex-shaped surface which reacts to sunlight. The polygonal segments of the surface react to ultra-violet light, mapping the position and intensity of solar rays. When in the shade, the segments of OR are translucent white. However, when hit by sunlight they become colored, flooding the space below with different hues of light. At night, OR transforms into an enormous 'chandelier', disseminating light into the surrounding courtyard, an atmospheric space for events and gatherings.

The hues generated by the photoreactive surface are therefore indicators of changes in weather and daylight, a dynamic architectural tool that can be used on building exteriors. OR means skin, shine, light or shade.

OR is the first time that photoreactive technology has been used on an architectural scale. The ecological structure is a step in exploring the possibilities of photoreactive materials in the fields of furniture and design. The beauty of OR is its constant interaction with the elements, each moment of the day is unique. Special software components have been developed in order to create the shapes and to generate the cutting schedules.

OR Project
21 Montpelier Street
London SW71HF
UK

www.orproject.com
E-mail: info@orproject.com

Index of products and projects